I0118145

LEADING CONFLICT:
HOW TO FIGHT AT WORK

JOHN BAILIE, PH.D.

Amodo Media
P.O. Box 352
Springtown, PA 18081-0353

Copyright © 2025 Amodo Media
All rights reserved, including the right to reproduce this book or portions
thereof in any form whatsoever.

First Amodo Media edition June 2025.
ISBN: 979-8-218-87067-6

To David G.:
You taught me that my head
would take me further
than my hands.

CONTENTS

APPRECIATION

Heartfelt thanks to Pam, Rick, Ted, and Susan who taught me that my heart would take me further than my head. And most of all, to "Coach Ho", who was there for me when I needed it most, and taught me that a man doesn't always win—but he never backs down from life.

Many blessings and thanks to Erin, Lauren and Alexis. You stayed in my corner and gave the best encouragement, editing and design expertise that any writer could hope for... Thanks for sticking with me in the deep rounds.

PROLOGUE

I was in third grade. I got off the bus at school and noticed a big fifth grader teasing another much smaller kid. The smaller kid had a significant stutter. The fifth grader was mocking him: "Wha- wha- wha- what's a muh- muh- muh- matter, huh?" Typical schoolyard bully fare for the time. But still, the younger kid looked devastated, shamed, and embarrassed. He was just standing there, taking it and crying. No one was doing anything. Most kids were just watching and some were laughing along. The fifth grader was a mountain of a boy. He had a good foot and a half on me and had a big round barrel chest and belly.

Puffing out my nonexistent chest muscles and little chicken arms, I decided to step in front of the little kid and say to the big fifth grader, "Hey! Leave him alone!" Oh yeah, I meant business.

The big kid says, laughing and looking down at me, "What the @&%! are you gonna do about it?"

I still remember the next few seconds in super slow motion. Seeing how tall this kid was, I knew I needed to go for a devastating body shot. I wound up, cocking my right arm back along my side like a gunslinger cocking his Colt .45. And then, *Boom!* I cut loose with the most powerful punch I could muster, my fist plowing into his midsection. However, due to his aforementioned belly and my puny arms, it was like punching the proverbial bowl full of Jell-O. My fist just went in, and in, and in. Actually, I don't recall ever hitting anything solid. I just eventually ran out of arm length as I went to full extension. Zero effect.

Next, I looked up and felt the fear coming on. He looked down at me, more surprised than anything, but in no way hurt. *Oh… crap…* was my last thought as he began to rain fifth-grader death and destruction upon my face with his meaty paws. That went on for a while. Thankfully, he eventually just tired (or got bored) and walked away.

With a face full of snot and blood, I dragged myself into the building and called my mom from a pay phone. It was picture day. My shirt was wrecked and my face was a lunar landscape of craters and welts. I told my mom that I was sorry but I ruined my shirt and we shouldn't spend the money to get my picture taken that day. She told me not to worry, the picture could be rescheduled.

I didn't get much sympathy for the beating. After all, I threw the first punch. Fair enough. A teacher who saw the fight took me to the bathroom to help me get washed up and then off to class. There was no additional punishment at home for me since I was technically defending someone else—something my parents appreciated. And that was the end of that. Different times.

I've always loathed bullies. I got into enough fights as a kid to know that I could fight if I had to, but I preferred to avoid them if I could. I wasn't always completely innocent. I might have thrown the first punch a few times. But I'd like to think that, given the culture of the time, if I punched someone, they usually deserved it. The fights that I, and my two brothers, typically got into were usually with neighborhood punks and other sundry miscreants. A couple of them made a career out of being idiots and eventually did some time in prison. These kids rarely sought fair fights. They would surprise attack or gang up on us. Being the youngest of my brothers, I was usually jumped by kids much older and bigger than I was. I lost more fights than I won. But I learned not to run away, which would have made things worse. I also learned how to keep my wits about me while under duress. Most of the time I wasn't really fighting to win. I was fighting to minimize the damage and dish out as much as I could in return. Believe it or not, that takes more thoughtfulness than dishing out a one-sided beating.

Early in my life, I thankfully realized that my wits would likely take me further in life than my fists. As I got older, I learned to "win" fights using my noggin and to avoid the worst sorts of people and situations in the neighborhood. On TV, I watched fighters like the "Easton Assassin" Larry Holmes and "Iron" Mike Tyson with rapt awe and became a lifelong fan of boxing. Like every kid who grew up near Philadelphia at the time, I ran the steps of the Philadelphia Art Museum while imagining Rocky Balboa there by my side. I raised my arms at the top of the stairs, danced in victory with the rest of the children on the field trip, and looked out on a gray city that never seemed to change.

Even then, I sensed what any great boxing coach will tell you: the ring is a metaphor for life. Most of us will never know what it's like to step into the "squared circle" and under the lights at the Garden or MGM Grand. No. The real fights in life, the ones that really matter, come with much less fanfare. Unlike a boxing match, they are often unscheduled. The rules aren't clear, and the stakes are much higher than a multi-million-dollar fight purse.

These unexpected moments come in a marriage, beside a hospital bed, and in the quiet moments when we turn our eyes to heaven and acknowledge that none of us can go the distance on our own steam. On a daily basis, the regular challenges of working with others is our gym. It's our ring where we get to practice how we'll handle the most important "fight nights" that life will unpredictably dish out. How we respond to those moments will make all the difference. As a great mentor once taught me, those moments separate the contenders from the pretenders. In life, "heart" is what enables a real fighter to go the distance. Like Rocky said:

You, me, or nobody is gonna hit as hard as life. But it ain't about how hard you hit. It's about how hard you can get hit and keep moving forward; how much you can take and keep moving forward. That's how winning is done!

As for me, I studied hard, excelled in school, and went off to college on an ROTC scholarship. I channeled my remaining innate aggression into football, rugby, running, and working the heavy bag in the basement.

I made a great career, a wonderful marriage, and a big, happy, and rambunctious Irish Catholic family. Thankfully, none of my four children have ever seen a street fight in real life. I worked hard to ensure that their biggest daily problem is getting to jiu-jitsu and baseball practice on time. Don't get me wrong; my sons and I enjoy a good fight—but always on ESPN+ or with fat padded gloves in the basement, not on the sidewalk.

However, growing up in a rough working-class neighborhood taught me a few things: One, getting punched in the face hurts; try to avoid it if at all possible. Two, you should be able to work with your hands if you have to, but work with your head if you're able to. Three, even if you wear a tie to work every day, you need to know how to fight.

INTRODUCTION

The single greatest driver of happiness and satisfaction in the workplace is the quality of your relationships. When we are strongly bonded to those around us, know that our voice and ideas matter, and feel efficacious in bringing those ideas to reality in a well-functioning team, everything else around "satisfaction" usually falls into place. This matters more to most people than money, benefits, and paid vacation days. Those things are important, too, but they pale in comparison to strong relationships and a dignified workplace community.

There's much out there now in management and workplace psychology literature on ways to proactively encourage the development of workplaces like the one I just described. I write about that as well. However, in my work as a consultant and CEO coach, I've noticed that there's very little training and support around the flip side of those issues.

Often, the things we hate most about work are also relational. Talk to someone who loathes their job. Ask them why, and most will talk about things that have to do with people, not systems or remuneration. They will say that there's a lack of trust, a bullying supervisor, gossipy cliques, or perhaps a few toxic personalities that operate unchecked.

Every leader needs to know how to build a positive and affirming workplace community. However, to do that well, you also need to be skilled in addressing the relational problems and challenges that interrupt the formation of the relationships we all crave. And you need to do this just as skillfully, strategically, and sometimes aggressively as you pursue the other things that matter in your work.

Like all arts, martial or otherwise, relational conflict has its own set of foundational skills. You're unlikely to learn them by accident. You didn't learn them in school. Some of them are not pretty or fashionable in a world where hurting someone's feelings can be a capital offense. However, possessing these skills is one of the factors that have always separated the managers from the leaders, the contenders from the pretenders.

MY STORY

I've had a very unique career path. I am a Family Business Consultant with Compass Point, LLC—a consulting firm that exclusively serves family-owned companies. My personal focus areas are strategy development, company culture, governance, and CEO leadership coaching. Prior to this, I was the president of the International Institute for Restorative Practices (IIRP) Graduate School. Over more than twenty years at the IIRP, I helped to create an international executive education, training, and consulting platform and an independent graduate school from the ground up. My colleagues and I have facilitated the creation of an emerging social science devoted entirely to the study of relationships and community. I regularly consult, publish, and present internationally on the topics of leadership, conflict, human capital, and organizational culture.

My studies have included literature, art, and military science at Norwich University, as well as leadership, accounting, and logistics at the US Navy Supply Corps School. I studied counseling at the IIRP Graduate School, theology at Moravian Theological Seminary, and management and leadership at MIT Sloan. I hold a PhD in Education with a specialization in adult learning from Lesley University in Cambridge, Massachusetts.

It's been an exciting journey. Beyond the résumé, here's the real story.

I've been a problematic military officer, an unprofessional labor agitator, a counselor for troubled teens, an emergency room crisis counselor, a school discipline coach for urban educators, a leadership mentor, an organizational culture consultant, and a senior executive. This work has taken me around the world and placed me in the middle of some uniquely tough situations. I'm also a lifelong super-fan and occasional student of boxing and MMA—more as a metaphor for life than any interest in getting punched in the head for a living. Reflecting across all those experiences, one thing has become crystal clear to me. I'm drawn to conflict like a moth to a porch light.

I've jumped again and again from the proverbial frying pan into the fire. Many times, I told myself that I should settle down and do some work that would be more peaceful and relaxing. Perhaps I'd become a botanist, a poet, or start a BBQ joint. I never chose to do any of those things, at least not professionally. I do make a mean smoked pork shoulder, though. Just don't ask me about my poetry. It's awful.

I don't know exactly how I got this way. I could describe some of my childhood experiences and unresolved personal conflicts. I'll discuss some of those topics in this book. I could dissect the inner motivations that have driven my lifelong fascination with human relationships. I'll do some of that here as well. But honestly, I just like the excitement and growth that the study (and practice) of conflict offers. It's what I do instead of riding motorcycles, skydiving, or alligator wrestling.

I've made an interesting and deeply satisfying career out of exploring interpersonal conflict in the workplace. I learned most of what I know through twenty years of direct experience helping leaders and organizations in need, often at the most challenging times. For me, the doing came first. The theory came later.

This book, and its companion blog (www.leadingconflict.com), is dedicated to translating my unique skill set and experiences into helpful resources for organizational leaders—in work and the rest of life as well.

LET'S GET READY TO RUMBLE

This book is not a scholarly endeavor. If you want to read my academic work, it's out there for your perusal. The goal of this book is to distill what actually works in real-life interpersonal conflict. An understanding of psychology is useful. Studying the dynamics of organizational change is helpful. Neurobiology is fascinating. However, constructs, footnotes, degrees, and a shelf full of books will not help you when you're eyeball to eyeball with life's most challenging people and situations.

Studying conflict is not the same thing as engaging in it. It's the difference between being a boxer and a fan. This book assumes you, like every leader, already know a bit about workplace conflict. Maybe you studied the topic in school or simply learned on the job. However, few of us have developed interpersonal conflict skills with deliberate focus and explicit practice—the way a boxer learns the "sweet science" of the ring. These skills aren't distributed by level of education or the letters behind someone's name. In fact, a cabby or server is just as likely to be an expert in these skills as a division head or senior vice president.

This book names these skills and helps you practice them on purpose. The main part of this book is organized into three "rounds," just as many amateur boxing matches are fought. Each round presents three core principles of leading conflict and offers skills, insights, and practice tips that will prepare you for the next round.

Round One covers how to overcome the fear of engagement. Round Two is about facing the toughest opponent on the planet, yourself. Round Three teaches you how to put all these skills together strategically and with intent. Sprinkled throughout are some key "fight tips" and stories that will help you float like a butterfly and sting like a bee in the messy world of workplace relationships.

If you're ready, lace up your gloves and start practicing the fundamentals; I'll be in your corner. Let's get to work.

ROUND ONE:
OVERCOMING THE FEAR OF ENGAGEMENT

OVERVIEW

I once attended a course on leadership and conflict management taught by two leading experts in the field at a prestigious university. They'd written books on the topic and published extensively. People were paying thousands of dollars to learn from them directly. They had each conducted ground-breaking research and had fascinating case studies to illustrate the concepts they were teaching. Then, a real conflict happened.

A fellow student raised his hand and shared, very respectfully and pro-fessionally, that he found one of the anecdotes shared by the instructors to be personally offensive. He asked the instructors to delve more deeply into the points he raised. Frankly, I didn't think much of the interaction at first. It seemed commonplace enough among professionals accustomed to being forward and frank with one another. The student didn't even ask for much, just that the instructors hear him and take a few moments to discuss the issue.

What followed was the experience that eventually led me to write this book. These two experts on interpersonal conflict froze like proverbial deer in headlights. They verbally stumbled, tried to justify themselves, tap-danced, backpedaled, and obviously tried to blow past the student's challenge and just move on. Again, the student respectfully pressed the issue and even tried to help them, "Look, I'm just hoping we can talk about real topics like this, not for me personally, but because we are all likely to face similar issues in our organizations."

"After all," the student continued, "this is a course on leadership and conflict. Can we practice some of the skills we're being taught?" Good question. In fact, it was *the* question: To what extent do we practice the skills and concepts we understand intellectually but struggle to deploy in real time when they're most crucial?

This cycle continued until the student was now justifiably ticked off and the instructors looked like they wanted to crawl into a hole. Every time they tried to "fix it," they only clumsily made the situation worse by continuing to dodge the question—no doubt exacerbated by the shame of publicly floundering in their attempt to put into practice the very skills they were teaching.

Eventually, a colleague and I gently intervened and, along with the student who started the "confrontation," helped to lead the class into the necessary discussion. To the instructors' credit, at that point they took a back seat and let the class engage in what turned out to be a very fruitful and interesting conversation. We ended by agreeing to some "norms" going forward around risk-taking and allowing challenging voices to be heard.

Afterward, my colleague and I took some time to process what the heck had just happened. Why did such a minor conflict nearly derail a course taught by experts in leadership? The instructors weren't phonies. They were legitimately accomplished. I have no doubt they truly understood the material they were covering. They had excellent case studies to share, many of which were drawn from projects they had directly managed.

While processing the experience over some frosty beverages at the local scholarly watering hole, my colleague and I realized something. We were undoubtedly learning quite a lot in the course, especially regarding adult learning theory, leadership research, and organizational dynamics. We were doing our best to be good students. However, we also saw that without deliberate practice in real-time, real-life, stress-tested interpersonal conflict, you could never really be sure if you could perform under pressure.

So why were my colleague and I able to perform quite easily what two leading academics in the field failed to perform under only modest amounts of duress? It wasn't because we were geniuses. We thought about our personal and professional bios.

Each of us began our professional careers working with delinquent and troubled children—young people who had committed serious crimes, struggled with various addictions, or had been diagnosed with significant mental and behavioral health challenges. In that environment, conflict was a daily if not hourly phenomenon and almost never predictable. He specialized in addictions counseling and working with sex offenders. I translated my experience working with troubled youth into becoming a school climate and behavior consultant for some of the roughest urban secondary schools in the US. I spent the better part of my twenties and thirties in some of the toughest neighborhoods in cities such as Philadelphia, New York, Baltimore, and Detroit. In many of those projects, the professionals were even more challenging than the kids! I loved every minute of it.

By this point in our careers, each of us also was leading organizations in which we had purposely embedded expectations that staff were direct, frank, and courageous in interpersonal engagement and risk-taking. My work increasingly focused on training adult professionals, internally as a senior leader and externally as a mentor and consultant to private organizations and executives. Our cumulative experience and that of many others eventually led to the development of a graduate school founded with the sole purpose of teaching these very concepts and skills. Having grown up in similar working-class suburbs of Philly probably didn't hurt either. We had both grown up around machinists and steel workers in similar neighborhoods and families where people spoke their minds and there was a distinct lack of effete pretense. Children weren't coddled, and every kid did not get a trophy.

None of this made us perfect leaders. We were attending this course to round out our academic grounding—and no doubt sand off a few rough edges as well. We had plenty to learn. However, what we did know how to do, even better (we were surprised to learn) than a few leading experts, was to wade into the uncertainty and fear that comes with conflict and perform under pressure.

This changed how I approach my work. I realized that head-knowledge about conflict, psychology, and leadership was not enough. Also, practice in-and-of-itself was not enough. If that practice was, as in the case of my instructors, almost always in highly controlled and proscribed environments, a leader could not be depended upon to perform in spontaneous and highly unstructured moments—in other words, most of human interaction. It's the difference between learning a formal karate "kata" (a stylized series of moves, punches, and kicks) and being able to fight back after being cold-cocked at a bar.

This led me to ask a few new and challenging questions. What if I had been approaching my mentoring and teaching around leadership and conflict all wrong, or at least backward? Concepts and constructs that were unlikely to be actuated under pressure were functionally useless to a leader or an organization in a crisis. What if leaders approached their conflict skills the same way one would approach learning how to fight, or other high-contact sports and activities?

I have a doctorate in adult learning. I know a lot of other PhDs, professors, academics, and consultants. But when I reflected on the impressive practitioners in the realm of interpersonal conflict, very few of these people came to mind. Instead, when I thought of those whom I would trust to walk into almost any intense, uncertain, or volatile situation, a very different list of people emerged. These folks were more likely to be addictions professionals, shop foremen, emergency and trauma workers, high school disciplinarians, waitstaff, secretaries and personal assistants who manage big personalities for a living. When I thought about it, the skill set evident in this group had more in common with combat soldiers, cops, and martial arts instructors than with academics.

If that skill set was essential to performing under pressure, what was it? Could I make it explicit? Could it be taught? If you weren't lucky (or unlucky) enough to have a biography that made you an expert "fighter," either literally or figuratively, could you train yourself to become a person who knows that they can, when others hesitate, wade into nearly any high-conflict situation, excel, and lead? The answer of course is, with the proper motivation, an emphatic yes. It's not easy. It's not for everyone. It's hard, but everything worth having is. Like Mick the trainer said to Rocky Balboa, "You'll not only know how to fight. You'll know how to take care of yourself outside the ring too."

CONFLICT: LOVE IT AND LEAD IT

Working with troubled youth and coaching leaders are similar endeavors.

I've done both, and I find it much easier to work with a drug-addicted or gang-involved teenager than with a CEO. Teenagers tend to be pretty blunt and upfront with their opinions, emotions, and motivations. Even with the "toughest" kids, once you learn how to get through the thick outer shell, you usually find a whole lot of raw emotion and realness. On the other hand, adults (especially professionals and experts in their field) typically have much more complicated methods to hide, mask, or otherwise obscure what's really going on inside. It's checkers versus chess. Sometimes it's checkers versus 3-D underwater chess.

Most people, whether a teenager or an adult, avoid conflict most of the time. This is completely understandable. Most of us don't want to make others feel uncomfortable. We generally want to keep the peace and seek to put out interpersonal fires, not walk into them or set them alight. Even in the world of conflict resolution and management, I have encountered large measures of conflict avoidance. Often, people desire to become peacemakers because they actually fear and dislike conflict, not because they are interested in it. This is also understandable.

The tendency to avoid conflict, or resolve it superficially, has evolved in human relationships for very good reasons. For most of our collective history, we lived in small tribal groups in close quarters, where group collaboration was literally a matter of life and death. If humanity has a superpower, it is our ability to cooperate in pursuit of a shared vision. The healthy group dynamics needed to collectively bring down a mammoth are the same ones you need to launch a successful start-up. Same people. Different tasks. And you can't conduct a successful hunt or build a company if everyone is always fighting. This is true.

However, to build a mammoth-hunting party or start-up team, there are a lot of interpersonal issues that need to be sorted out. What role will each of us play? How will leadership be exercised and by whom? Will my experience be valued in this group? Will I have a voice in things here? Do I like and want to spend time with these people? Do I have the necessary skills to be of help? If not, how hard am I willing to work to develop those skills? How much am I willing to personally sacrifice in pursuit of this vision? The list goes on.

Every group, whether at home or in the workplace, must sort out a similar list of questions. That cannot happen if the group habitually avoids conflict. In fact, the highest performing groups learn that they need group members who are willing to lead conflict—not just manage it or resolve it. Real conflict, the truly useful kind, is messy, chaotic, and can be scary. But within the roots of conflict flows the lifeblood of creativity, possibility, self-knowledge, and group evolution.

WHY YOU NEED MORE FIGHTS AT WORK

Contrary to what you might think, you need more fights at work—not fewer.

Conflict is good. Conflict exposes our needs, desires, commitments, and fears. Conflict shows us where we are strong and where we are weak. Conflict is the path to personal and organizational growth. For all these reasons, conflict should not be simply resolved or managed. Conflict should be led. This is an essential skill for would-be transformational leaders like you.

Learning how to "fight" at work is not about behaving badly, being hurtful, or causing chaos for its own sake. It is about knowing how to lead others through the chaos of interpersonal conflict and find meaning and growth in the mess. However, along with snakes, public speaking, and heights, few things are more terrifying to normal people than the prospect of interpersonal conflict. Like these other phobias, most people will do nearly anything to avoid conflict—especially in the workplace, where relationships are often not as safe or secure as those in your private life.

You likely work with a great number of people who are not your friends, you did not choose to hire, and with whom you will likely never socialize outside the office. You might even have incredibly productive and successful work relationships with people you don't even particularly like!

The intimate web of shared history, vulnerability, and identity present in our personal relationships can make private conflict intense, but also safer and more familiar. We take risks more easily with our intimates. These factors are rarely present as consistently, if at all, in our workplace relationships. This makes conflict at work feel very risky. Contrary to what people say in the moment, most people fail to confront a colleague, not because they "don't really care" or because "it's no big deal" but because it's scary to do so with people you actually don't know very well and to whom you are only very loosely bonded.

The result of this conflict avoidance is that the conflicts that do boil over at work tend to be toxic and destructive ones that have festered for far too long. They often become toxic and destructive because multiple people (maybe you among them) saw the conflicts coming and either didn't know what to do or chose to do nothing in the hopes that the situation would magically get better on its own. That almost never works.

Time doesn't actually heal physical or relational wounds. Only proper care and attention heals wounds. Time is your friend only if you are applying an effective treatment. Neglect plus time can equal a deadly infection in a physical wound. Neglect plus time with relational wounds can multiply misunderstandings and enable the most toxic personality tendencies to dominate.

You need more "fights" at work because most conflicts are avoided when they are at the stage at which a mild treatment might prevent a nasty infection. You need more small conflicts that are effective, creative, and short in duration.

Except for a few weirdos like me (and maybe you), most team members are unlikely to enjoy the conflict when it's happening. So, even if it's a very creative and constructive conflict, it's best to keep things moving. Highly effective teams do not wallow in their strife or obsess over interpersonal dynamics. Instead, the best teams learn how to cycle rapidly through highly productive and creative conflicts and then move on to the next challenge and task.

But what if you were the one person in nearly every work-related situation who was most comfortable and confident leading conflict? In the midst of conflict—while others were running away, melting down, or boiling over—what if you knew exactly what needed to happen and had a plan and the guts to do it? You would become tremendously valuable to that team. Regardless of your actual title, you would become a transformational leader that people would always want near them during critical moments and conversations. However, everything worth having requires effort, pain, and sacrifice. Learning to lead conflict is no different.

DON'T MANAGE CONFLICT—LEAD IT

Managing is about overseeing processes, plans, and systems. It's about keeping things, often created by others, running. Leading is about engaging and becoming immersed in the nuanced and complicated lives of real people. Leading is envisioning, building, and sometimes breaking things on purpose. Leadership manifests ideas and aspirations.

Management and leadership skills are both essential for a healthy organization, but they are not the same thing. In some organizations, the assignment of these tasks is rigid and highly concentrated into specific job roles. A nuclear power plant has a very high percentage of people whose job it is to manage a finely tuned system of fixed processes and procedures. Within a cooperatively run organic farm, things might be a little more fluid.

There are a limited number of people in any organization who are explicitly assigned managerial tasks. However, the great thing about leadership is that anyone can lead.

Some roles have strong leadership expectations baked into them. However, the most effective organizations expect some amount of leadership from every role—from the part-time intern to the CEO. The roots of conflict lie in the small things that happen in relationships and communication: the gaps, nooks, and crannies of workplace behavior. Accordingly, high-quality responses to conflict do not lend themselves well to centralized and hierarchical management. When building a high-performing team, it is crucial that conflict leadership skills be widely distributed across the culture, regardless of role and position in the official hierarchy.

If you want to maximize the benefits of conflict, you need to help those directly involved learn to lead conflict themselves, instead of giving specialists the job of managing it from afar.

It's the nature of the management role to seek stasis and stability. Managerial tasks are oriented around efficiency and risk avoidance. Usually, this is precisely what is needed to oversee a supply chain, monitor a large investment, or execute a five-year strategic plan. Those tasks are usually explicitly assigned to people who excel at them.

The nature of the leadership role is to create uncertainty, challenge existing practice, and look beyond what is, toward what is possible. These skills can and should be practiced by anyone. You can lead conflict regardless of your title.

The skills discussed in this book are not only for people who have "conflict *something-or-other*" in their job description or work for human resources. These skills are meant for you and the challenges you face in workplace relationships every day. The following chapters will help you lead conflict by:

- Seeing conflict as necessary, not a disruption
- Engaging conflict, not suppressing it
- Maximizing the benefits of conflict, not avoiding risk
- Expanding participation, not isolating those involved

Do this, and conflict becomes more than an opportunity for your team to grow. It becomes an opportunity to lead.

TOXIC VERSUS CREATIVE CONFLICT

Many years of experience as a leadership coach and organizational change consultant have proven one fact to me again and again: *The presence of open conflicts within a work team, along with leaders who are skilled at managing it, is a sign of group health and an indication of that team's potential to perform beyond normal expectations.*

The mediocre team seeks calm, avoids conflict, and keeps the peace. The high-performing team pushes boundaries, exposes contradictions, and raises difficult interpersonal questions that often cause temporary friction among team members.

Instead of settling for the immediate gratification of conflict avoidance, high-performing teams sacrifice short-term peace for long-term results. This willful delaying of gratification and the conflicts that accompany this delay are signs of team maturity—not dysfunction.

All workplace conflict is potentially fruitful. However, there are two broad categories of conflict that happen within teams that must be understood in order to provide effective leadership: creative conflict and toxic conflict. Both types are similar on the surface. But each requires a very different response and skill set from leaders.

Creative conflict is rooted in the *dynamics between people.* In creative conflict, the motives and goals of group members are typically quite similar, healthy, and ultimately oriented toward a desire to solve concrete external problems and challenges. For instance, a team of engineers might have two camps within it that each envision a very different solution to a technical challenge. There might be strong leaders who passionately argue each group's position and engage in very distinct and intense conflict. Things might even boil over a few times before the issues are resolved. However, although the conflict involves strong personalities, it is not ultimately personal. The conflict is rooted in a sincere and shared desire to solve a real and pressing external challenge. The creative conflict is part of the team's path to performance and cohesion.

Toxic conflict, on the other hand, is typically rooted in the *personalities of individual people.* Toxic conflicts are rarely about the problem or challenge that is being presented on the surface. While creative conflict is rooted in an external problem, toxic conflict is rooted in one or more individual personalities and the dynamics between them and the group. The personality-driven causes of toxic conflict can be conscious or unconscious, intentional or simply instinctual, depending on the type of personalities involved. For instance, in the same team of engineers mentioned earlier, we might see similar disagreements over an ostensibly technical challenge. However, rather than driving toward a creative resolution to that external problem, the conflict consistently diverts into nasty personal attacks and issues unrelated to what's being discussed on the surface.

While creative conflicts might be uncomfortable, they tend to be remembered as productive periods in the life of the group that helped them evolve positively as a team. In contrast, toxic conflicts are often draining and confusing episodes that can destroy the long-term ability of a group to perform. To prevent this from happening, the group needs courageous leaders willing to confront and assist the individual personalities at the center of toxic conflict. Overcoming these difficult challenges and personalities successfully will also be remembered as an important milestone, but one that involved much pain, risk, and effort.

To lead creative conflicts, focus on giving the team time and space to work out the issues with as much autonomy as possible. Make sure there are clear opportunities for all voices to be heard—perhaps through the use of practices such as restorative circles or fair process (see www.iirp.edu). It is often useful to help such groups develop some basic conversational ground rules and norms that encourage a real discussion of issues and risk-taking within agreed upon behavioral boundaries. Lead creative conflict by helping the group collaboratively address the problem in a way that is respectful and honest.

Improve your ability to lead creative conflict by learning to facilitate emotionally risky group conversations and proactively establish group norms without taking over or imposing fixes.

To provide leadership during toxic conflict, leaders must be willing to expose and confront the personalities (i.e., individual people) at the root of the conflict. This does not mean that these people should be treated poorly or shamed. The presence of such personality issues, though difficult, is common in every organization. But as a leader, you must be willing to pointedly help those generating toxic conflict to examine their behavior patterns and motives, as well as how they are impacting the group.

In extreme cases, persistently toxic personalities that prove unwilling to examine or change their behavior might need to be reassigned or otherwise removed from the team. If there is a real external challenge that needs to be tackled, the group won't make much progress until the behavior of these individuals is confronted and their negative impact minimized. You waste group energy when you avoid addressing an individual personality problem. It is generally easier to engage an external creative conflict than a more nebulous and risky toxic conflict. However, effective leaders must know how to tell one from the other and be willing to practice the different responses that each requires.

Improve your ability to lead toxic conflict by learning how to confront individuals directly, challenge behavior while not denigrating the individual, and take immediate decisive action in the best interests of the group.

PRINCIPLE 1:
MOVE TOWARD FEAR

Interpersonal strategies don't amount to much if your first instinct is to run away from conflict—or, more accurately, the fear that conflict produces.

You must develop the unnatural habit of moving toward fear, not away from it. Millions of years of human development have ensured that a wide range of alarms go off in your body and mind when things aren't going right between you and other people. We are all hardwired to connect to others, to seek meaningful relationships with like-minded people. When stuff happens between people to impede this, humans respond in fairly predictable ways.

You might lash out at others, avoid the situation, run away, or even blame yourself. Your breathing tightens. Your pulse quickens. Your mind might race or feel paralyzed and blank. Your vision narrows and blocks out all but this one important thing: the event, the person or people in front of you right now.

This is the physical experience of conflict. Your body and mind both limit and heighten your attention and senses to ensure that you are focused on what your biology perceives as a threat. It doesn't matter if the threat is physical or psychological; your bodily responses will be similar. Even for the interpersonal adrenaline junkies among us, this reaction is never really experienced as pleasurable per se. However, there's a certain heightened awareness that comes with this type of focus. It's like the pins-and-needles before you rush onto the field at the start of a sporting event, or the coiled alertness of a linebacker waiting for the center to snap the ball. Over time, you will learn to appreciate the "flow" that's possible within that space. And it's that flow, that only comes with competence, repetition, and lots of practice, that can feel pretty amazing. It's precisely that same in any other art—the jazz clarinetist before a big solo, the actor waiting in the wings for their defining scene, the paratrooper before they dive into an inky night sky. It's the act of becoming instantaneously present—of fully occupying the time and space in front of us right now, right here. In that place, fear cannot control us.

The experience of conflict always involves some measure of fear and discomfort. It is learning how to face and use that fear that, at a certain level of expertise, can provide meaningful positive experiences. You can't eliminate the fear, but you can ensure that it is not your master. Notice that I didn't say that you can "master fear." The goal isn't to master fear. Fear is useful, normal, and natural. Fighting fear is not a productive use of time and energy. Instead, you must practice simply recognizing fear and seeing it for what it is: just another emotion and range of bodily reactions. Fear will control you only if you let it.

Don't fight fear. Make friends with it. Learn how it works in your body and what it is trying to tell you when it happens. Fear, properly utilized, is a wise advisor—not a dictator. After you understand how fear works, you must understand how you personally respond to it. While the core experience of fear is fairly universal, we each react to it a little differently. Our own life history and experiences have a large impact on how we make sense of conflict. You likely come to this book with deeply ingrained reactions and assumptions about conflict. By the time you make it through childhood, adolescence, and young adulthood and then join a team of adults in a work setting, you are guaranteed to have a pre-existing pattern of behavior around the experience of conflict.

Take some time this week to think about how you personally respond to conflict and fear. Do you want to run away? Tend to blame yourself? Do you lash out? Or maybe you avoid and try to distract yourself. Learn to recognize your instinctive reactions. Listen to them. Pause to reflect on what happened to cause this reaction. Perfect the small habit of pausing, reflecting, and not running away from the fear. Then, take one or two immediate actions that bring you closer to what happened instead of running from it. For instance, you might immediately share how you are feeling with the person in front of you, tell your team that what is happening is not OK, or schedule that meeting with a colleague that you have been avoiding. Don't worry about fixing things yet or being eloquent. Just take some small action that helps you step toward the conflict instead of away from it. Over time, moving in and taking action will become easier and more instinctual. As one of my mentors taught me, action cures fear.

FIGHT TIP

PLAN TO BE SPONTANEOUS

When learning how to move toward fear, it's key to immediately take one or two actions to move closer to the situation, rather than run away from it.

One way to do this more strategically is to plan to be spontaneous. A contradiction? Not really.

Chances are, most problems and issues that you have with colleagues are not isolated instances. They recur again, and again... and again.

Since you know your colleague will likely repeat the same behavior in the future, have a clear plan of action and commit to following through with it the next time the behavior is repeated.

It is important to plan actions that you can take right there, in the moment, when the behavior occurs. Your response is likely to have more impact the closer it is in time to the actual incident.

Consider sharing your plan of action with another trusted friend or colleague. This accountability will help you follow through (i.e., not chicken out). You can also process with them afterward.

This way, you get to both plan ahead and react spontaneously in the moment.

AGAINST CAUTION

Most of what passes for conflict management/resolution wisdom and education is far too cautious and avoidant and, frankly, fails to address the root issues inherent in most conflicts. This is because the human desire for interpersonal peace is so strong that most leaders will purposely or inadvertently suppress a conflict far too soon in its life cycle. The reasons for shutting down or "resolving" conflict too soon usually come from a good place.

Much of the existing practice in the world of conflict management/ resolution caters to the desire for peace and conflict suppression. We don't want to see people in discomfort. We want things to be "OK" again. This is fine if you want an organizational culture that is only OK. But it's the wrong approach if you want a culture that is truly great.

People and relationships are far more resilient and robust in their potential to absorb conflict and change than leaders usually give them credit for. Staff can handle it—really. It is usually the leadership, not the staff, who keeps a lid on useful conflict that needs to come to the surface. In my years of educating, coaching, and leading, I've learned that there is more inherent downside to the things that go *unsaid* in an organization than for the risky things we choose to say out loud. Organizations that encourage interpersonal risk-taking are not for everyone. That's because most organizations, and leaders, are rather mediocre.

You didn't come here to read this because you want to be mediocre. You want to be exceptional. Transformational leaders will do what is necessary to make sure that things that need to be said get said.

Model creative risk-taking with your team this week, by experimenting with the following:

1. Trust that if you are thinking something, especially something that makes you uncomfortable, someone else is thinking it too. Be the first to say it out loud.
2. Talk to a colleague about a problematic and persistent behavior— one that you've complained about to everyone but them (or just kept to yourself).
3. Be more OK with things not being OK. Many interpersonal issues cannot be resolved in one conversation or meeting. Don't insist on fake and superficial conclusions. Be willing to talk more the next

day or on a regularly scheduled basis about issues or behaviors that might be deeply ingrained.

Practice the above, and you'll start "moving toward fear" like a champ.

FIGHT TIP

SAY THAT THING

Be a model of creative risk-taking this week. How about this:

Like I suggested earlier, talk to a colleague about a problematic and persistent behavior—that you've complained about to everyone but them (or just kept to yourself). Sounds intriguing and very healthy, right?

Easier said than done.

For all the reasons discussed earlier, it's scary to confront co-workers that you actually don't know very well compared to your loved ones.

So here are a few steps to help you say that thing that needs to be said:

Schedule it. If you waited this long to be honest with your colleague, it's not just going to happen. Get the conversation on both of your calendars—today.

Tell them what it's about. Don't leave the person wondering what this meeting is about. If it is going to be a difficult conversation, just tell them what you plan to talk about. For instance, "I want to talk about what happened at the meeting yesterday. I've been feeling upset about it and want to process this with you."

Start by admitting this is difficult for you. Even if you are an expert at faking unshakeable self-confidence, these conversations are always hard. Start by telling the person that this is hard for you and that you care about them (or at least their performance), which is why you are taking the time to talk directly. Tell them they are worth it. This builds empathy and should help you feel more comfortable. Honesty about emotions de-escalates feelings of fear and apprehension.

You can do it. Say that thing.

HOW TO TAKE A PUNCH AT WORK

When you like a sport as much as I like boxing, it becomes more than a hobby. It becomes a metaphor for life. My favorite part of boxing isn't actually the fighting. I'm fascinated by the psychology of the fight. I'm intensely interested in the personal stories behind each fighter and what drives them to endure the punishment of the ring. Some boxers love the art of the sport, the "sweet science" as they say. Some love the money or the fame. But some boxers actually just enjoy getting punched in the face.

Don't believe me? Watch some old interviews with the famed Boston-area boxer "Irish" Micky Ward. The real lives of Micky, his brother Dicky (also a professional boxer), and their nutty Irish family were chronicled in the 2010 film *The Fighter*, starring Mark Wahlberg as Micky and Christian Bale as Dicky. But honestly, the real-life Micky Ward is infinitely more fascinating.

Micky liked getting punched in the face.

Micky was known for his ability to absorb incredible amounts of punishment and keep on fighting. He was the real-life Rocky Balboa. For boxing fans, his "toe-to-toe" brawling style meant breathtaking edge-of-your-seat fights. It wasn't pretty. His fights were often brutal and bloody slugfests. Micky didn't float like Ali the tactician. He wasn't elusive like Mayweather. He mostly stood directly in front of his opponents, who were often more technically skilled, and just started throwing fist-bombs. He also started absorbing them.

He never ran away and was willing to stand face-to-face, round after round, with men that should have terrified him. Sometimes he won. Sometimes he didn't. But no one left a fight with Micky unscathed. His career record of 38 wins (28 by KO) and 13 losses won't impress many casual fans. But die-hard boxing fans don't love Micky for his record. They love him because he had incredible "heart" and an inhumanly iron chin. Micky was a great boxer because he loved the essence of the sport in its brutal simplicity.

Like Micky, you can learn to like getting punched in the face (metaphorically speaking). In the context of leading conflict outside the ring, you need to be careful. You just might start enjoying yourself. In boxing training, it takes a while to learn how to move, how to throw a proper punch, and how to take one. Even when you're wearing lots of safety gear and only going three-quarter speed, sparring can be intimidating at first. Even people who've been in lots of street fights have to learn how to fight off tunnel vision and panic, relax, and be purposeful in their choices and movements. Expertise takes time. There are no long-term shortcuts to competence.

When you work hard at mastering a skill set, inside the ring or out, there's nothing wrong with taking pleasure in deploying those skills. Once you get over the apprehension and anxiety around conflict, you'll be ready to up your game. You'll be able to think in the middle of the chaos of the "ring." Over the next few sections, we'll start layering the skills you'll need to lead conflict at work.

Micky accepted and learned to relish the scariest part of his profession. He wasn't immune to fear, and I'm sure it hurt like holy heck when he took a hard left hook to the jaw. But Micky learned to love, as great boxers do, developing the skills to operate, survive, and thrive in an inherently hostile environment.

So how do you take a punch at work? Well, unless you're a professional fighter or a thug for a loan shark, I hope that actual fisticuffs are not a regular part of your day. Most "punches" at work come in the form of criticism and confrontation from colleagues and supervisors. Leading conflict is not just about throwing punches. You also need to know how to take them.

Here are a few simple strategies that will help you take the next punch that comes your way.

Thank the person for confronting you. What? Are you crazy? *Thank* the person? Yes. I am a little crazy, but I'm also serious.

After the person is done with their initial confrontation or criticism, you should say something like this: "Thank you for talking to me directly. I really appreciate it and I'm sure that was difficult for you." Bringing concerns to someone directly takes courage, and that deserves to be acknowledged—even if you totally disagree with the content of what they are saying.

Then listen. Really, just listen. The hardest discipline to learn is when to shut your trap. The person you just thanked needs to know that you are actually hearing them. In fact, this is typically 80 percent or more of what they actually want from you—to know that you've heard them. They might not be fully aware of it, but it's true. Remember the story I shared in the introduction? If the presenters had simply listened, acknowledged the feedback, and committed to reflect on it, they would have had a much easier time and maybe learned a thing or two from the student.

The more someone feels listened to, the less they will ask of you during and after the confrontation. The conversation itself will give the person most of what they need. This will save you time and energy in the future.

When people are in the midst of being confronted, they typically send a barrage of physical and verbal cues signaling that they cannot wait to speak, retort, tell their side, and talk over the other person. These cues always escalate the conversation, because they make the other person afraid that they are not being heard.

My mentors excelled at simply listening to people. Often, even when they could have argued or challenged the other person, they would simply wait in silence during pauses in the conversation and then ask, "Is there anything else?" Sometimes the other person would say a little more and sometimes not. The other person always looked a little confused at first, but in a good way. After all, they likely came into the room ready to brawl. But…

First, they were thanked. And then, the other person just listened and didn't argue with them. This strategy is disorienting because the listener is not following the expected script that assumes they will be resistant to hearing or granting any requests.

Ask what they need from you. Next, simply ask something like, "What is it that you need from me?" Encourage the person to be specific. They are not likely to have thought about this before they confronted you. You might need to help them get concrete. If you don't understand what they are asking of you, be sure to ask for clarification. Don't patronize them. Say something like, "I want to make sure you get what you need. Can you say more about X?" Or you might need to say, "Can you tell me more about what that would look like?"

You can ask someone what they need from you even if you don't completely understand everything that brought them to you in the first place. Instead of challenging and dissecting every detail in their version of events, it is sometimes a better use of your time to simply ask them what they need. At this point, you are actively helping them receive something that they thought would need to be extracted by "force" and argument. Honestly, sometimes people just thank you for listening and don't ask for anything else.

Make sure you both have a clear understanding about what's next. Simply repeat your understanding about what needs to happen now and/or how things will be different in the future. That's it. Don't rehash earlier parts of the conversation. Thank them again and let things end at this point.

This simple framework is especially helpful when you feel panicky or have no idea how to respond to someone. That's kind of the whole point. You don't need to have all the answers. The other person does most of the work.

Also, this is a pretty good summary of how you want people to respond when you confront them, right? Well, if you want your colleagues to learn how to take a punch, you need to show them how it's done.

FIGHT TIP

IF IT DOESN'T APPLY, LET IT FLY

As I said in describing "how to take a punch," you can ask someone what they need from you even if you don't completely understand everything that brought them to you in the first place.

Instead of challenging and dissecting every detail in their version of events, it is sometimes a better use of your time to simply ask them what they need.

This takes practice. When you disagree or feel defensive, you naturally want to argue and push back. And sometimes we should.

But often, the person sharing feedback with us is simply giving their perception of events—or perhaps their perception of you personally. That's valuable. There's no real right or wrong, other than how you feel about the information.

In these cases, just listen, and if it doesn't apply, let it fly.

Liberate yourself from the need to constantly defend yourself against criticism. Just thank them and think about what they shared with you.

Even a few days later, you might find something important worth considering in their feedback, something that you weren't really hearing during the conversation.

TOXIC WORKPLACE BEHAVIOR PROFILES

Previously, I discussed one of the key features that distinguishes toxic conflict from creative conflict.

Creative conflict is rooted in the *dynamics between people*. In creative conflict, the motives and goals of group members are typically healthy and focused on a sincere desire to solve concrete external problems and challenges.

Toxic conflict is typically rooted in the *personalities of individual people*. While creative conflict is rooted in an external problem, toxic conflict is rooted in the problematic behavior of one or more individuals.

Toxic conflict is hard on a team. Thankfully, most of the behavior that generates toxic conflict is common and predictable.

This means that you can plan ahead for behaviors that are certain to recur. Think of these Toxic Workplace Behavior Profiles as your top-secret files on how to prepare and respond strategically to the most disruptive and toxic behaviors in your workplace.

THE SUBMARINE

Code Name: The Submarine
Motto: Run silent; run deep.
Favorite Song: "Every Breath You Take" by The Police (Feel free to play in the background while reading.)
Favorite Movie: *Das Boot*
Behavior: In naval warfare, the role of the submarine is to stay hidden and silently stalk those in the sunlight above from the black depths below. It is the same with the office Submarine.

The Submarine smiles and nods politely in meetings. They say hello every morning, maybe even pausing to compliment your fetching sweater.

But then, the Submarine submerges...

The Submarine is the one who says nothing during the brainstorming session but then criticizes ideas, plans, coworkers, and leaders through gossip and innuendo. They target other impressionable coworkers to influence, but never openly. Their undermining and critical conversations take place at the watercooler, in the parking lot, and during the after-hours social gathering.

The Submarine isn't toxic because of their criticisms. They're toxic because they never share those criticisms openly, in the appropriate forum, or with the person who can actually do something about them.

Also, the Submarine draws otherwise healthy colleagues into its dark and watery lair by ensnaring them in frequent negative conversations, often marked by gossip and personal attacks on other coworkers. Consciously or not, the Submarine uses these conversations to manipulate others into colluding with them, even if others do so with hesitation. Without assistance from leaders, it is very difficult for coworkers to break away from the Submarine's secretive pattern of behavior.

The Submarine lowers morale, undermines plans and decisions, and creates silent factions in the team.

As in naval warfare, unless you are proactive and plan ahead, you are not likely to know about the Submarine's presence until the damage is done.

Do Not: When dealing with a Submarine in the workplace, there is one thing you must never do. Do not engage in sub-on-sub warfare. Do not play the Submarine's game by going into the silent deep with them. They are better at fighting from the shadows than you are—and generally willing to play much dirtier than you will. Sure, sub-on-sub warfare sounds exciting, but it frequently ends badly for everyone.

Do: As soon as you suspect a Submarine is at work, you must make its presence known publicly and keep it on your radar. My brother spent the last decade of the Cold War hunting and tracking Soviet subs from the air. Using radar and a net of underwater listening devices, his goal was to keep constant contact with these hidden Russkies. The ocean is a great place to hide, but it's not a great medium in which to maneuver quickly. Once you have a sub targeted and tracked by surface and air assets, it is far less deadly and much easier to neutralize.

At work, use team meeting time to talk about the responsibility to raise concerns openly *and* with the person who can do something about them. If approached with toxic conversation at the watercooler, how do you handle it? If you are getting sucked into secretive complaining, what do you do? Talk about these things on a regular basis. Let the team brainstorm how to handle these common problems and temptations.

As a leader, you must intentionally role-model what this looks like and plan to do this as a regular part of your team leadership. These norms will ultimately limit the space in which a potential Submarine can operate.

You cannot completely eliminate the operating area of a Submarine, but you can make the environment inhospitable.

When a specific Submarine is personally identified, or even suspected, you must confront them. The chapters that follow will help you overcome the fear of these conversations. You will almost always be operating on partial information or just a hunch. This is fine. You don't need—or want to spend the time to create—an airtight case. Simply approach the person with curiosity and questions.

Probe more than you accuse. Problem-solve more than you judge.

If they admit to Submarine-like behavior, compliment and thank them. Admitting to toxic behavior takes courage. Then, help them share any ideas and legitimate concerns openly and in the most effective forum.

If they are just complaining and gossiping, tell them they need to stop, insist on a plan of behavior change, and make this a regular topic in supervision until you're confident the behavior has ceased.

Consider using group processes such as circles to encourage these colleagues to process their past behavior publicly and share their plan for change with the team.

Humility check: Though some people habitually engage in this behavior, you have probably behaved this way at some point as well. If so, consider sharing this with your team; then tell them what you will do to not repeat this behavior in the future. Role-modeling this type of risk-taking will be a powerful example to others of how you expect them to respond when confronted about the same behavior.

PRINCIPLE 2: THERE'S NO NICE WAY TO POKE SOMEONE IN THE EYE

When I began my career as a professional educator and trainer, I was young, arrogant, and stubborn. Now I'm just arrogant and stubborn. One day, I was co-training a group of professionals with my supervisor. He was an experienced consultant, trainer, and a top-shelf presenter. He was a truly gifted speaker and mentor who could work a room like nobody's business.

During a Q&A session, one of our trainees asked an insightful question about how to give tough feedback without permanently damaging a relationship with a coworker. It was an excellent question. After playing second-fiddle for most of the training, I felt I had some original ideas. I was excited to finally speak up.

My supervisor answered first and gave a few concise pieces of advice. I then shared my ideas. However, I also decided to go the extra mile and disagree with one of my supervisor's comments. I gave some clear supporting reasons and then made a contrasting suggestion.

He responded by gently reiterating his point and giving a further rationale for his original suggestion. Though he gently tried to make a transition to the next activity, I decided to double down on stupid by going back to my point and making it more strongly this time. We went back and forth a few times before I finally realized things were getting tense—and awkward for the trainees. We clumsily moved on.

After the training, my supervisor tried to process what had happened. He explained that he didn't have a problem with me having a difference of opinion or even sharing it with the group. He explained that he, knowing the particular trainees much better and more intimately than I did, had very distinct reasons for giving the particular advice he had shared. The advice was related to some much larger development goals he had established with the trainees' organizational leadership.

He asked me to trust his judgment and follow his lead in situations like this in the future, at least until I learned more about our clients' history and goals. All very sensible, strategic, and professionally delivered feedback on his part. And what did I do? Yep, I told him why he was wrong—again.

The next day at the office, I was asked to come to a meeting in one of the conference rooms. As I walked in, I saw that there were four chairs arranged in a circle. In three of the chairs were my supervisor, our unit director, and the president of the company. The empty chair was for me.

My supervisor asked me to come in and have a seat. I was told that they all wanted to talk to me about what happened at the training on the previous day and—for now—they just wanted me to listen. My supervisor reiterated his points from the previous day. He also added how frustrated he was with me. He said he was devoting a lot of time to help mentor me, but I was often resistant to advice. Next, the president of the company said he'd like to speak. After a thoughtful pause, he looked at me seriously and said, "I put your supervisor in charge for a reason. He is our most experienced and talented trainer and consultant. I've worked with him for more than ten years, and I trust him completely. If I wanted you in charge, you'd be in charge. From now on, you follow his lead with clients whether you agree or not. You're a smart, talented guy with a lot of potential. But you can also be arrogant and hard to teach. If that doesn't change, you won't make it here."

I felt like I was punched in the gut. And it was exactly what I needed and deserved.

Our unit director then talked a little bit about the potential she saw in me, but she also shared some related concerns. I was then asked to share what I would explicitly do differently from now on in similar situations. They helped me develop a few clear commitments. Then we ended the meeting.

It was hard for me, but I did what they asked and followed through on my commitments. And I learned a lot about myself in the process. The number one thing they did right was not pulling any punches. As a colleague of mine is fond of saying, "There's no nice way to poke someone in the eye."

If they had even mildly sugarcoated the feedback or phrased everything as polite suggestions, I frankly wouldn't have heard it. And I wouldn't have changed. I needed to be told I was wrong and that while my opinion might be valid, it wasn't the most important one in the room. It was great that I wanted to lead, but first I needed to learn how to follow with grace. And if I didn't develop in this area, I'd be gone.

That was all true. I needed to hear it straight—no chaser. Feedback often fails to make an impact or change behavior because it's overly diluted. Wrapping feedback in cautious niceties helps only the giver, not the receiver. Sometimes, people are just wrong, like I was in this situation. And if you need to poke them in the metaphorical eye, it's best and most effective to just get it over with as quickly as possible. Then you can get on with making things better.

FIGHT TIP

FEEDBACK SANDWICHES TASTE TERRIBLE

Some of you might have been taught the "sandwich" method of giving feedback. This method attempts to put something critical (the meat) between two compliments (the bread). As I said previously, strategies like this help only the giver, not the receiver.

In fact, what will happen over time is that when you give a colleague a compliment, they are likely to think, "Uh oh, here it comes…" because you've trained them to think a criticism or confrontation will follow. Bad practice. Doesn't work. If you do this, even unconsciously, stop.

The sandwich was popularized because it helped people feel like less of a jerk for confronting someone—not because it was an effective feedback method.

Instead, just tell the person what they need to hear and get it over with. If necessary, it is sometimes helpful to lead with, "I need to talk to you about the meeting yesterday (or whatever the issue is); this is hard for me." (Only acknowledge that this is hard for you if you need to.) Then give the undiluted feedback.

Be humane. Be empathetic. But be direct. Let your criticisms be critical. And let your compliments be complimentary.

EMPATHY IS OVERRATED

Empathy is overrated. I know this is heresy to modern sensibilities. Before you light your torch and grab your pitchfork, hear me out.

We live in a world suffused with psychological language. Even in fields that are not traditionally considered to be "touchy-feely," leaders are likely to be expected to know how to increase their team's emotional intelligence, help employees build emotional self-management skills, or increase a sense of belonging and community.

In part, this mirrors the positive development of the field of psychology as a whole. As we understand more about the mind of the human person and how we relate to each other, we apply those insights to a wider range of settings, such as workplaces. On the other hand, we have also seen the rise of popular psychology and an entire industry related to self-help and pseudo-scientific ideas about emotion. These ideas are often based on what we wish were true about people, instead of the reality of how human beings are actually wired. One perfect example is the perceived role of empathy in conflict.

The ability to understand another's feelings and thoughts from their point of view is a great skill. Honing your ability to do this will help you make more nuanced decisions and relate to others with more tact and sensitivity. Here's the problem: empathy has become an idol, a panacea, a magical thing that promises to end all conflict and allow leaders and staff to exist on a higher and more sensitive plane of existence.

As I've discussed already, most people seek to avoid conflict. Accordingly, popular pseudo-psychology has encouraged the belief that if we just had more empathy we'd have less conflict. So, we don't need to do the difficult work of confronting people about their behavior, which is really unpleasant and scary. We just need to start empathizing more! After all, unlike leading conflict, empathizing makes me feel great about myself and is less risky. Problem solved! I exaggerate, but not by much in the case of some leaders and workplaces.

Empathy is essential to healthy human relationships, but it's not a cure-all. The presence of empathy does not negate the need for boundary-setting and does not necessarily lead to behavior change. Simply empathizing changes nothing. Behavior change requires pressure, concrete plans, and a willingness to move beyond talking about feelings and into action. Expression of empathy is a good beginning to a conversation, but it's not an end unto itself. Empathy is only one good among many in the list of leadership skills and competencies. An overemphasis on empathy in leadership can lead to a reluctance to cause others discomfort. After all, if you *really* empathized with others, you wouldn't want to cause them discomfort, right?

This is a serious problem in many workplaces. As a leader, a big part of your job is to make other people uncomfortable on a regular basis. Being uncomfortable is a natural part of learning and the development of expertise. And as a leader, you should be the teacher-in-chief before you are the empathizer-in-chief. Be an empathetic teacher, not a teaching empath.

Overplaying the importance of empathy can also lead to the erroneous belief among colleagues that they should never be made to experience difficult, negative, or uncomfortable feelings. Here's an example from my personal life: I once confronted someone I was close to about their pattern of manipulatively using anger, threats, and histrionics during conflict. I discussed how scary, difficult, and damaging this behavior was for me and others.

The response from that person was, "How can you say these things to me? How do you think it makes me feel when you tell me things like this?" To which my response was, "Well, I assume you feel bad. And that would be appropriate." We are no longer close. And that's a good thing.

The most effective leaders are empathetic to those around them in a general way, while also being able and willing to cause discomfort to others as needed. Growth and learning require some amount of pain and sacrifice.

None of us feels what everyone around us is feeling at all times, nor should we. That would be really exhausting and unhealthy. We understand the feelings of others. We care about the experiences of others. We listen to others. But their feelings are their feelings, and our feelings are our own. How to make sense of that information and what you do with it is what matters most when leading conflict.

FIGHT TIP

EMPATHY IS NOT AGREEMENT

Being empathetic does not mean protecting people from discomfort. Discomfort is the thing that most often leads someone to change. But there's an even bigger error that can be made.

Sometimes, these same colleagues have been led to believe that empathizing with them means that you must therefore agree with their perspective or co-sign their behavior. Nothing could be further from the truth.

Empathy does not imply agreement.

You can empathize with someone's experience, feelings, or particular and unique situation. You can also simultaneously disagree with that person's conclusions and disapprove of their behavior.

In fact, your ability to empathize is most important in those cases where disagreement and disapproval are most needed. This will help you reject harmful behavior while affirming their worth as a person.

For instance, if a colleague accuses you of insufficient or false empathy because you still disagree with their ideas or behavior, you might say something like this: "I'm sure that this has been difficult for you. I really appreciate you sharing this with me directly. I do believe that you want to address the situation. I have some ideas that might be challenging for you and that I think might help. Can I share them with you?"

There is nothing in that language that negates their subjective experience or difficult feelings. In fact, you are clearly saying that your challenge to them is rooted in your empathy for them.

SAY MORE THAN "NO"

What do you do when your organization asks you to do something unethical? A leader I was coaching recently posed that question to me. They were facing a tough situation. Their supervisor was informally pressuring them to falsify performance data for certain people served by the institution. Part of them wanted to run away from the situation—maybe even quit. However, they decided they had a responsibility to address the core ethical issue at stake. They asked for some advice.

Of course, you can simply follow Nancy Reagan's advice on avoiding temptation and just say no. But sometimes, there are opportunities to say no in a way that helps the organization learn from the experience and regain its ethical compass. It is somewhat easy to just say no to an unethical temptation when you can walk away from the situation. But temptations to do the wrong thing usually come from the people closest to us—whether a friend, family member, or colleague. And when you can't just walk away from the situation, you need to say more than no. I shared a story with my client.

I once worked as an emergency room crisis counselor for a large mental health organization. We routinely served people with severe mental health and/or substance abuse issues. Our patients were often suicidal, high on drugs, in the midst of withdrawal, or experiencing some manner of acute psychosis. They were lawyers and laborers, housewives and people experiencing homelessness. You never knew who would show up or what situation might present itself during any given shift.

We met people in the most unstable, extreme, and volatile periods of their lives. Our job was to take it as it came, treat people with dignity, and get them the help they needed. We sometimes played a role in recommending temporary involuntary commitment when someone was an active danger to themselves or others. In these cases, we occasionally needed to call hospital security if someone was a flight risk or posed a threat to staff or themselves.

None of the counseling staff were trained or certified in restraint techniques, nor was this a part of our job description. However, one of the crisis counseling staff supervisors began requesting that we physically restrain patients if they attempted to leave without permission and security wasn't there to stop them.

I understood why the request was being made. There had been several patient "escapes" that required police intervention in the surrounding neighborhood and had garnered media attention (i.e., mental health patients running down the street in hospital gowns while being chased by the cops).

The local community was becoming concerned about safety. This was damaging the institution's reputation. There was tremendous pressure from above to improve security within the crisis unit of the emergency room. I was unwilling to agree to the request, which I considered to be both ethically and legally unsound. However, I wanted to respond in a way that also acknowledged that there was a real problem in need of a concrete solution.

In a staff meeting with the team and supervisor, I asked a series of questions:

- Is restraining patients a part of our job description as crisis counselors? (The answer was no.)
- Has anyone on the crisis staff been formally trained and certified to perform these types of restraints? (The answer was no.)
- Given those facts, are you requesting that we restrain patients anyway? (The answer was very confusing and muddled.)
- Can you explain how the organization will manage the liability in the case of a lawsuit by an injured patient? (The answer was, "I have no idea.")
- Given the above, does it still seem fair or wise to request that untrained staff restrain patients? (The answer was, "I suppose not...")

The supervisor then said, somewhat frustrated, "Well, just make sure that you request a security presence if you even suspect a patient will be volatile or might flee."

That was the correct answer and led us into a more nuanced discussion about how to collaborate and communicate more effectively with the security staff, which was the real crux of the issue. Security typically complained if they were called to the unit when there wasn't an immediate crisis. Yet, security often arrived too late once a patient decided to bolt for the door or otherwise cause chaos. After a few tough meetings between the security and counseling staff, we sorted things out and largely solved the problem. I also thankfully avoided having to tackle patients on the hospital lawn.

Sometimes, there is tremendous pressure to do something that everyone knows is against the rules or ethically questionable. The next time you are in this position, consider how you can ask challenging and reflective questions that put leadership in a position that pressures them to either:

- Admit plainly that they are asking staff to do something unethical or against policy, or

- Slow down and find another solution to what is likely a real problem that deserves a more thoughtful solution.

Unethical decisions often begin as an attempt to provide a quick solution to a real problem—moving away from fear. When this happens, slow things down. Use reflective questions to move toward fear and help the team not take the easy way out of a tough situation. Be challenging *and* supportive. Whenever possible, say more than no.

FIGHT TIP

YOU CHOSE THESE PEOPLE FOR A REASON

When you work around a lot of relational "racket and chaos," it's easy to start feeling pretty negative about the people around you. At times like this it's important to remember that you chose to work with these people. Every day that you show up and walk through the door, you make that choice again.

You're not a victim. You're here by choice. You picked these people. They picked you too.

Reflect on why you chose to spend so much time with them. You had a reason, but you probably haven't thought about it in a while. There was something you thought they would bring to your life, something you hoped to learn from them, or something you believed you could do together that you could not do separately.

Before you react to the chaos, remember those things. Write them down. Post them somewhere that will remind you that these people have value. Be the one who remembers the reasons you are all together, and others will remember too. Only then can you really help in a way that makes things better and doesn't just add to the noise.

PUNK-UP YOUR FEEDBACK AT WORK

I loved '80s punk music when I was kid. OK, I liked some '90s punk too. No, I'm not talking about Green Day. *American Idiot* was still a fun musical though. I was never really a full-fledged punk myself, but I always had a few punk friends in my social periphery as a teenager. I guess I was kind of a "punk tourist," if that's a thing. After I left the military in the mid-'90s, I found myself sharing rent in several admittedly sketchy collective living situations with lots of real punks.

What's that like?

Imagine the movie *Mad Max* stuffed into a small apartment where no one takes out the trash, there are no defined sleep schedules, and there are weekly full-size concerts in the living room. Oi! Oi! Oi!

I never jumped into the mosh pit of punk-world with both feet. However, I was made an "honorary punk" by a guy named Scooter. Scooter kind of looked like Joey Ramone's evil-er twin. He was about a buck-forty soaking wet and six-foot-two, plus another one whole foot of perfectly straight Elmer's-glued purple mohawk. Seriously, Elmer's glue is the secret to a perfect hawk. There's also a method that requires a blowtorch and belt sander. But don't. Really. Don't. In fact, if you still have a mohawk and you're reading a book about leadership and workplace conflict, it might be time to grow up. It's at least time for a new hairstyle.

Most of the punks I lived with claimed to be anarchists, so they couldn't admit to having leaders. But I suspect that Scooter was the unofficial punk king, kind of like being king of the wildlings north of the wall. So, I suppose he had the power to dispense honorary-punk titles and privileges.

Alas, those days are long gone. I now enjoy quiet nights reading, healthcare, and a shower with plumbing that actually works. What does this little walk down the memory lane of punkdom have to do with leading conflict at work? Imagine a whole flat filled with folks like Scooter. Now imagine that you are the only one who actually cares if the garbage is taken out, people are practicing remedial hygiene, and everyone is making at least a token rent contribution. Oh yeah, there's also some dude that no one seems to know who's been sleeping in a closet every night for over a week. True story.

In an environment like this, you get lots of practice in confrontation and figuring out how to be heard when those around you are used to day-to-day racket and confusion. If this is how you feel at work sometimes, here are some tips on how to get heard above the noise:

Pull the plug. Sometimes the sheer pace of things in a busy organization takes on a life of its own. The flow of work and the conflict between people can start happening so fast and furiously that it's easy to become reactive when you need to be strategic.

This can make a leader feel like a firefighter in a room full of children with matches. As soon as one interpersonal fire is put out, five more have started. When things feel out of control, you might need to stop everything, get everyone to drop what they are doing, and ensure that you have their full attention.

If people can't hear you over the band's lightning-fast power chords, screaming into the mic, and horrible distortion from the four amps someone stacked on the coffee table, you need to pull the plug and stop the show. Punk music sounds ridiculous without high-powered distortion. Office conflict is the same. They'll stop and listen if you kill the power.

In the office this means: close your laptop, put away your smartphones, cancel your next videoconference, and let the landline go to voicemail. We all need to talk. Now.

Stand next to the dead rat. If things in the office have been messed up and chaotic for a while, people might hate it, but they also tend to get used to it.

In one of my living situations, the state of the kitchen was my number one headache. It wasn't just messy; it was a public health threat. The kitchen was so bad that after many attempts to lecture everyone about the growing array of fungi and other hazards, I started lining the counter with giant rat traps. These were not the friendly live-capture traps available today. They were the old, brutal spring-loaded snap-traps. Within a day, we had a giant dead rat on the counter.

My assumption was that this gruesome spectacle would inspire a spasm of dishwashing and tile scrubbing. One day passed. Then two days. Another day passed as the rat was becoming a rotten zombie-rat. I now had the perfect concrete example for our next house kitchen discussion.

Talking vaguely about kitchen cleanliness in the abstract was not very effective. Doing so while standing next to a three-day-old rotting rat did make an impact. Though to be honest, a couple of my roomies actually said they were sad to see the dead rat go. It was "pretty punk" after all. Sigh…

Whenever possible, don't discuss problems in the abstract. Provide a real and immediate example of what results from poor performance or behavior. Quality leadership is also part theater. Use your props wisely.

Repeat yourself, while upping the ante. If you've been droning on and on about the same problem for too long, people eventually stop listening. You might need to up the ante.

Pull the plug to ensure you're being heard. Stand next to the metaphorical dead rat to ensure that what you're talking about is real and concrete. You might need to do these things more than once. Just make sure that the consequences for not changing go up with each repetition.

Some consequences are natural. The stench of the dead rat was only going to get worse if everyone chose to do nothing.

Other consequences might need to be imposed. One night, the weekly punk show in the living room was so out of control that I threatened to call the cops on my own apartment. This was a decidedly un-punk thing to do. It was also effective.

Conversation, collaborative engagement, and banking on empathy doesn't solve every problem. There is a selective and strategic role for the fear of consequences. If used sparingly, fear can be an effective motivator of last resort. You can't fight noise with more noise. So, the next time things feel out of control at work, lace up those Doc Martens and get creative. Strategizing how to actually be heard is just as important as knowing what to say.

TOXIC WORKPLACE BEHAVIOR PROFILE

THE BRUTUS

Code Name: The Brutus
Motto: Sincerity—If you can fake that, you've got it made.
Favorite Song: "Back Stabbers" by The O'Jays
Favorite Movie: *The Ides of March* (R.I.P. Philip Seymour Hoffman)
Behavior: The O'Jays said it all in their super-smooth '70s hit "Back Stabbers": "They smile in your face... All the time they want to take your place." If Julius Caesar had only watched more *Soul Train*.

Whether the Brutus wants to take your woman, your man, your corner office, or the last cruller in the break room, their behavior will always revolve around one simple principle: they use intimacy and trust as weapons.

The workplace Brutus is very difficult to handle because we don't want to believe that they exist. After all, most of us greatly value trust, loyalty, and friendship. The thought of weaponizing those basic building blocks of human relationships is inherently repellent.

We have all violated someone's trust at some point in our lives. But the idea that there are those who do so habitually, purposely, and with strategic forethought is a hard reality to accept.

Most people's first response when they suspect someone is a Brutus is to explain away the behavior as a misunderstanding or even self-induced paranoia. The Brutus knows this and will often double down on their deception by playing on your feelings of guilt for even suspecting them in the first place.

The Brutus will say things like:
"It's all a misunderstanding."
"How could you even think such a thing?"
"I would never do something like that to you."

The Brutus is not simply ambitious. Highly ambitious people might, rightly or wrongly, throw a few elbows now and then to get ahead. The Brutus is different.

The Brutus is motivated by both ambition and an extreme and toxic form of covetousness. They don't just want to get ahead or achieve something. They want what *you* have. In fact, the Brutus is convinced that they *should have* what you have.

This person usually has a strong and compelling narrative in their head. In this internal story, they are not a villain. Instead, they are actually the hero. They might believe they've been wronged, passed-over, or unrecognized. Perhaps they feel more competent, smarter, or harder working than others who have greater status or prestige in the organization.

The Brutus broods: Why should you have *that* position, *that* promotion, *that* kind of attention and praise from the boss? After all, your success is really due to something the Brutus has provided that has gone unrecognized. In this narrative, the Brutus is justified in taking these things from you. In fact, justice demands that they do so. They are not betraying you. They are setting things aright. It is this inverted hero-narrative that motivates the Brutus and provides them with a justification for lies and betrayal.

Interestingly, this is precisely the mix of characteristics that intelligence operatives look for in potential turncoats and defectors. It explains why people sell secrets to foreign governments and why Greg stole my Star Wars action figures in fourth grade. (You know what you did, Greg.) If you are going to convince someone to betray their country, comrades, and family, you need to help them not despise themselves for it. An intelligence handler will encourage the person to tell themselves a story in which they are the hero and all their problems in life come from others, not from within. Unlike those motivated by greed, the Brutus will often do this kind of espionage work for free. It is the internal story that drives them.

Tragically, these motivators and personality characteristics also tend to doom the Brutus's plans from the beginning. They might experience some temporary successes, but it is precisely these personality flaws that often impair the Brutus's ability to advance in the first place. The mundane workplace Brutus tends to find themselves again and again in the same toxic and destructive patterns—never quite achieving the object, status, recognition, or vindication they want.

They consistently fail in their attempts to solve internal problems with external solutions.

Even if they do achieve a position of leadership, the reign of a Brutus is typically unstable and short. Eventually, they learn what successful people already know: you cannot truly rise by cutting other people down.

Do Not: The only way to never be hurt by a Brutus is to mistrust everyone. That will do more damage to your life than anything a Brutus could ever do to you.

Accept that someone with whom you are very close will betray you at some point. Most of us already have such a story in our lives. Do not stop believing or trusting in others. Don't fall prey to paranoia or start thinking, like a mob boss, that every subordinate is a potential threat.

Most people, though flawed, are not a Brutus. When most people betray a confidence, or do something selfish for their own gain, it is impulsive and situational, not strategic and habitual.

Do: That being said, you need to know the signs that someone might be a Brutus and what you can do if someone is betraying your trust in the workplace.

First, consider this simple rule of thumb from the greatest espionage author of all time (OK, besides maybe John le Carré), Ian Fleming. Call it Fleming's Law. Sir Ian said, "Once is happenstance. Twice is coincidence. Three times is enemy action."

As discussed previously, betrayal by a Brutus is systematic. It will take place more than once, in different ways, and over time. When that happens, you need to take notice, take action, and confront the Brutus. When you do confront a Brutus, focus on cold facts and not unprovable allegations. Facts are your friend and will keep you sane when the Brutus doubles down on their deception.

The Brutus will evade and try to explain away their behavior. They will attempt to make you question your own perception of events. They will offer an alternate false narrative that is sprinkled with just enough truth to make it plausible. They will try to make you feel like you are taking crazy pills. In response, you need to be steady and resolute. You should sound something like this: "No. This is not a misunderstanding. You told me one thing. You told Sally another thing. And then you lied about it—just now. You have done this repeatedly."

It helps to have other supporters who can back you up during these conversations. The Brutus is a practiced manipulator and will attempt to split any group that confronts them. Talk about this with your supporters before the conversation. Ensure that you all share the same perception of events and goals for the conversation.

If you discover that a potential supporter sees things differently, hear them out. But do not have them in the room when you confront the Brutus. Otherwise, the Brutus will use that person's doubts against you. In short, when dealing with a Brutus, trust Fleming's Law. Focus on the facts. Gather supporters. Do not be distracted by evasion. State the truth with force and confidence.

As Philip Seymour Hoffman says when he confronts betrayal in the movie *The Ides of March*, "No, Stephen. You didn't make a mistake. You made a choice." *Boom!* Study Mr. Hoffman. Be one with Philip Seymour Hoffman the next time you confront a Brutus.

PRINCIPLE 3:
EMBRACE
THE SUCK

In 2010–11, I was a little overwhelmed. Things at work were as busy as ever. I was a year into my doctoral studies and heading toward my comprehensive exams. My wife was pregnant with our first son.

I was also processing the deaths of several family members over the previous five years—two of whom were cousins around my age. One died in a motorcycle accident. The other took his own life while in the throes of grief over the death of his brother. To complete the country-western song, I had recently put down my aging dog, Seamus the pug. So there was good stuff happening, and there was hard stuff happening. But it was, to say the least, a lot.

The natural and healthy response to all of this was of course to decide that it would be a great time to start training for a marathon. Not just a marathon—how about a *trail marathon*? Wait a minute, how about a trail *ultra*-marathon? My wife, knowing just how deeply disturbed I am, thankfully did not intervene. She let me deal with things in my usual odd and over-the-top way.

Surely, there was some avoidance going on here. Overwhelmed by events, my response in part was to pile on more activity. However, I was also using a skill I was taught as a young man in the military. The therapeutic term is "embrace the suck." Sometimes events overtake you. These are often events you can't control, like deaths in the family. But there are also circumstances you choose and need to own, like starting a PhD program, having more children, and committing to a ludicrous running event.

About the running: When you run fifteen miles into the wilderness, feeling broken, drained, and racked with pain, you eventually realize that there is only one way out—the way you got in. You need to embrace the suck and keep running. Doing this on purpose, in a setting I chose, helped me cope with the circumstances I couldn't control in my life at the time.

I learned the same lesson on long road marches in military school. Regardless of how you feel, the only way to make it stop is to finish it. Keep putting one foot in front of the other. Keep moving forward. Eventually, it will be over.

Whether on a road march, in an ultra-marathon, processing grief, or leading conflict, success begins with accepting that the process includes suffering. The more you can accept that and embrace it, the better you will do. Leading conflict with colleagues requires that you develop the habit of moving toward fear and get used to poking people in the eye, metaphorically speaking. You do these things because they need to be done. And being the rare person who can do it is very satisfying. That's what you are working toward.

The next time you need to confront someone, have a hard conversation, or make people uncomfortable by challenging existing practice, own the process. Wade in. Embrace the suck.

FIGHT TIP

RUN TO THE NEXT ROCK

As I say in this chapter, you don't lead conflict because it feels good; you do it because it needs to be done. Success begins with accepting that the process includes suffering. The more you can accept that and embrace it, the better you will do.

That being said, what do you do when you are in the crappy part of conflict, the "suck" part? Again, the ultra-marathon analogy is helpful.

When you set out to run a ridiculous distance for no logical reason, you do not think about and count down the total miles. You do not say to yourself, "One mile down. Only 32 more to go! Three miles down. Nearly 10 percent finished!" Do that and you will fail. The idea of finishing, the massiveness of the task, will quickly become overwhelming. You will likely quit. You'll quit because your mind will give up before your body has reached any actual limit.

Instead, you focus on running to the next reasonable milestone. Maybe that's the next aid station a few miles away. Later in the race, when you *really* want to quit, you might need to focus on running to the next big rock only a few yards ahead. Then another milestone. Then another.

The only time you should think about the finish line is when you cross it.

Do the same when leading conflict. Don't think about the end when you are at the beginning, or in the middle. Focus on the next thing you need to do and do that thing to the best of your ability. Then the next thing. And so on.

Do that, and you won't get overwhelmed or chicken out. Like my first ultra-marathon, you might finish ugly and near the back, but you will finish.

PRACTICE YOUR LISTENING STANCE

One of the first things you practice when you learn a martial art is how to stand and position your body for action. As I said previously, most "punches" at work come in the form of criticism and confrontation from colleagues and supervisors. Leading conflict is not just about throwing punches. You also need to know how to take them. And if you're going to take a workplace "punch" correctly, you need to practice your stance. In particular, you need to practice your listening stance. This might sound (and feel) a little awkward at first—but trust me, it works.

Besides actually paying attention, the second most important part of listening is that you look like you are listening. Most of this is accomplished with body language. It sounds simple, but it actually takes a lot of deliberate practice. Here are the basics:

1. **Relax.** At least, you need to look like you're relaxed. For instance, I have what some have called a "resting business face." This is a nice way of saying that if I'm not careful, I can look angry and overly intense when I'm just thinking, focused, and paying close attention. What do I do to get my face into a "listening stance"? I open my eyes wider, unfurrow my brow (which has a mind of its own), and unclench my jaw. Basically, I purposely undo anything that reads as aggressive or tense.

2. **Put your body into an "open" position.** Whether standing or sitting, do not fold your arms on your chest. Let your arms sit naturally in your lap. Do not make fists. If there's a table, keep your hands visible and open. Casually lacing your fingers is fine. Roll your shoulders back in order to "open up" your chest and midsection. Our chest and abdomen contain our vital organs. We cover them when we feel threatened. Uncovering these areas subconsciously demonstrates trust.

3. **If standing, it's best to lean back on something like a wall or table.** This signals that you are not in an "action ready" mode. You're cool and relaxed. It's all good. You are ready to have this super-productive conversation—even if you're freaking out inside or dying to check your watch because you have *that* meeting in ten minutes...

4. **If sitting, do not lean forward.** I know you think this makes you look interested and earnest. But to someone who is nervous and afraid

that you will argue with them, it just reads as aggressive. Leaning into space, closer to the person talking is a subtle way to exert will and dominance. There's a time to do this. That time is not now. Sit back in your chair. Relaxed slouching works as well. Just try not to look bored—especially if you are.

5. **Smile.** But do it genuinely. Fake smiles are worse than not smiling at all. Practice a relaxed and content semi-smile. Think gentle and approachable, not patronizing.

If you do the above, the other person should sense that you are open, attentive, and ready to hear what they have to say.

Once you get really good at moving into your listening stance, you'll have to work to avoid what frequently happens when my wife finishes talking and says something like, "So what do you think?" To which my reply is too frequently, "Ummm... yeah. I'm sorry. Can you say that again? I totally wasn't listening."

FIGHT  TIP

TIME IT!

We've already covered how to make sure you look like you are listening when someone confronts you or gives you feedback. The five easy tips covered in this chapter will make sure you appear ready and willing to hear everything your coworker has to say.

But what if you have an important meeting in a few minutes? What if you have a meeting you were supposed to be at two minutes ago?

One of the most common reasons we send verbal and nonverbal cues that we are not really listening to another person is that we feel pressed for time. We have other responsibilities. We planned to spend the next ten minutes doing something else (like preparing for the impending meeting) other than having this unexpected conversation.

The best way to handle this is to take control and time it.

Agree to talk only for the amount of time you actually have in that moment and during which you can give this person your full attention.

It should sound something like this:

If your coworker Pete asks to talk to you and you have a meeting in ten minutes, say something like, "This seems important. I have a meeting in ten minutes and I need about five minutes to prepare. Is this something we can talk about in five minutes or less, or do you need more time?"

If you do not have time now, say something like, "I can see this is important. I can't talk now because I am already two minutes late for a meeting, but I want to make time for this. Can I stop by as soon as my meeting is over and set a time for us to meet?"

Be just as specific as the examples above. Even though it might feel weird at first, it's the specificity that makes it work.

Don't say:

"Is it quick?"

"Is it important?"

"Is it urgent?"

"Do you really need to talk now?"

"I'm kinda busy now; can we talk later?"

All those common phrases are likely to send the message, intended or not, that what Pete has to say is not your biggest priority. Those questions also imply that Pete needs to figure out the right time to talk to you, which is kind of impossible. He's likely to just feel blown off.

Instead:

1. Assume that what the other person has to say is important and say so.
2. Tell them exactly how much time you do (or do not) have right now.
3. Agree to an explicit additional amount of time (and the place) to talk further if needed.
4. Stick to the agreed time limit.

Then, actually give the person your full attention. Be fully present. Do not multitask or keep glancing at your texts. Put your phone away and on silent. Close your laptop.

Do that conversation once, right, and fully—so you don't have to do it twice.

CHEERFULNESS IS A CHOICE— AND A WEAPON

Happiness is a feeling. Cheerfulness is a choice—and a weapon.

By cheerfulness, I don't mean schmaltzy niceties and fake smiles. Real cheerfulness means something much deeper. Cheerfulness is the ability to willingly, even gladly, bear the slings and arrows of life and relationships. The feeling of happiness comes and goes like weather. Cheerfulness can be deliberately chosen and cultivated as a virtue in leading conflict.

The ability to be willfully cheerful in the face of adversity is a powerful weapon. It's not a weapon against people. Individual people are never really at the heart of any problem.

Instead, cheerfulness is a weapon against the real enemies in life: discouragement, despondency, faithlessness, despair. Deliberate cheerfulness allows us to stand our ground when all seems dark, the odds are against us, or relationships turn sour.

When relationships falter, our initial reactions are often a mixture of sadness and anger. There is nothing wrong with sadness. It's natural to feel sadness in the face of loss or disappointment.

Anger is often the appropriate initial reaction in the face of injustice or other offenses against what is right and expected behavior. Anger can help us to move out of the paralysis of sadness and into action. Anger might be a great motivator, but it's a terrible tactician. You must move beyond it to lead conflict effectively.

There's a great old quote from the US labor movement: "Beware of a movement that sings!" The meaning of this phrase is, once roused by righteous anger, successful movements are those that find the heart and hope to gladly suffer for something larger than themselves, not for the destruction of enemies but for their transformation. For instance, the US civil rights movement and the struggle to topple Soviet Communism in Europe were causes separated by time and culture. However, both shared similarly buoyant leaders who inspired hopefulness in the face of terrible injustice and violent repression. In the micro-context of relationships and workplace conflict, the same lessons hold true.

You can lead conflict effectively only when you are committed to something larger than your personal comfort. That might be your care for the well-being of the person in front of you, the culture of your organization as a whole, or the mission your institution serves.

You must know who you are, what you stand for, and why you are willingly facing the discomfort that comes with conflict. This is essential. Otherwise, we will simply seek solace in the limited selfishness of our own personal happiness—just "making it through the day."

Choosing to be cheerful means you are willing to free yourself from what is convenient to you and experience suffering for the sake of others. The ability to do this is the ability to lead others through conflict.

Beware. It's easy to imagine ourselves being self-sacrificing in large and showy ways. This is comfortable because it feeds the ego. It also allows us to put off sacrifice for a later day. It's much harder to choose cheerfulness each day in the innumerable small things that no one notices.

In the coming week, try out a few of these tips to practice cheerfulness on a small scale:

- Make time to talk with a colleague you normally avoid. Learn something about them you did not know. Share something personal with them that you normally wouldn't.
- Take a week off from complaining about being busy or having too much on your plate. When someone asks you how things are going this week, choose to share something that you or others (even better) are doing well.
- Offer unexpected encouragement to five colleagues, one for each day of the week. Make a schedule and an explicit commitment to talk to a specific person each day.
- Don't tell anyone what you are doing or seek any praise for it. Just do it because it's the right thing to do.

The most powerful weapons don't hurt; they heal. And those weapons take a lifetime to master. So, don't delay. Start practicing now.

STAY IN THE PROBLEM

Humans loathe uncertainty. We like patterns, routines, and structure. We like knowing what's going to happen next. Even creative pursuits, like jazz or abstract painting, that seem to thrive on a lack of structure are really made interesting because they bend expected structural expectations. In the enjoyment, there's still a strong relationship to the expectation of order and the underlying classical "rules" of the art form.

When the mind encounters disorder of any kind, it immediately attempts to organize the data and produce a structure that will give the mess meaning, make it intelligible, categorizable, and controllable. A Pollock painting or a Coltrane riff is interesting because your mind attempts to draw meaning and impose order on something spontaneous, loosely structured, or even chaotic. But if an artist moves too far away from established expectations and rules, the work risks becoming actually meaningless. Music becomes noise. Art becomes trash.

The same process is at work in conflict. When we encounter a relational mess, we are hardwired to feel uncomfortable. Like the person staring at a Pollock painting, when we encounter relational conflict, we know things are not in their right place. We sense the disorder and fear it. If only subconsciously, we fear that the relational glue that holds us together will dissolve and leave us alone and unconnected—a very primal anxiety. However, our emotions drive us to impose order when faced with conflict. We are literally compelled by our hardwiring to set things right and resolve tension in relationships.

In workplace conflict, the real danger is not that our relationships will completely fall apart. That is actually quite rare. The real danger is that, in response to the emotional tension surrounding conflict, we resolve things too superficially and too soon.

Instead, teams must learn how to *stay* in the problem.

During a lecture at the MIT Sloan School of Management, the great management professor Ralph Katz once referred to this uncomfortable experience as "the problem space." Most bad decisions, whether technical or relational, arise from a team's inability to stay in the problem space—their inability to embrace the suck and turn it into something useful.

In short, teams respond too quickly to the emotional tension and begin taking action far too soon.

You can help your team stay in the problem by:

- Providing permission to NOT fix things (i.e., not too fast)
- Removing obstacles to participation in the conversation (e.g., carve out time; give people permission to make this a priority; let other tasks slide if needed)
- Helping them frame the right questions, not the right answers (e.g., measure success by the quality and completeness of the engagement, not by how fast things are "fixed" or even the particular outcomes)

To lead conflict effectively, avoid moving to actions and resolution, until:

- The conversation includes those closest to the problem
- There is a shared understanding and definition of the problem itself
- All potential options for action are understood and digested by the group

Leading conflict creatively requires that you generate uncertainty by surfacing tensions, then manage that uncertainty by using these guidelines to help your team stay in the problem until they are *really* ready to act.

Until then, learn to love the mess.

DON'T BE RESILIENT; BE ANTIFRAGILE

The opposite of fragile is not resilient; it's "antifragile."

We all know what fragile means. It is something that's easily broken, delicate, and must be treated with great care and caution. While we might greatly value fine objects with these qualities, such as a beautiful stained-glass window or a treasured porcelain vase, no one wants to be a fragile person.

In the quest to avoid fragility, the common wisdom is that one should develop resilience. We usually think of resilience as the ability to withstand and recover from the onslaught of life's troubles and conflict. If the fragile person is made of porcelain, the highly resilient person is made of iron. However, is resilient really the opposite of fragile? Essayist and risk analyst Nassim Taleb says no.

My favorite philosophers and thinkers are not the ones who propose wholly novel concepts. The things that are most true in life are fairly easy to understand but hard to practice. Similarly, Taleb's book *Antifragile: Things That Gain from Disorder* proposes a simple idea and then proceeds to think through its challenging consequences. The idea is this: If fragile things are damaged by stress and risk, the opposite of fragile would be a thing that is actively strengthened by exposure to stress and risk. That thing, or person, would be "antifragile."

This is very different from the idea of resilience as a measure of "robustness" in the face of danger. Applied to people and relationships, fragility and resilience share a similar underlying assumption. More accurately, they share the same desire. Both the person who fears their fragility and the person who seeks to be more resilient live in opposition to forces of risk, change, and uncertainty. One is easily broken. The other is more resistant to damage. Ultimately, both fragility and resilience imply that the ideal is a steady state of existence, an equanimity that is less disrupted by outside forces. That might not be what everyone means when they reference "resilience," but that is often how it plays out in popular practice.

The antifragile person is another matter entirely. This type of personality actively strengthens under duress. The antifragile leader might not actually enjoy risk, but they have developed the ability to purposefully thrive under uncertain conditions that others simply seek to withstand or avoid. Imagine that intense interpersonal conflict is a hurricane. The fragile person is broken by the storm. The resilient person stoically stands within the wind and resists the chaos. The antifragile person is strengthened by it and dances within the gales of uncertainty.

Leading and embracing conflict does not mean liking pain or causing conflict for its own sake. That would be abnormal and unhealthy. However, building skill in working within conditions that naturally evoke fear and avoidance requires a mindset that actually strengthens and blooms under those conditions.

Here is some practical advice to help you go beyond the quest for resilience in leading conflict and move closer to becoming antifragile:

Regularly expose yourself to measured amounts of interpersonal risk. Use small opportunities every day to practice putting the leading conflict principles into action. Speak up instead of being silent in meetings and supervision. Walk down the hall and talk to the colleague with whom you've had a disagreement instead of sending an email or putting it off until next week.

The key here is to practice a little bit each day, but not overdo it. On a risk scale of 1 to 10, it's better to take regular risks between 1 and 5. Excessive risk-taking between 6 and 10 will burn you out and drive other people a little nuts. Be judicious and balanced. This will build your tolerance for risk and make interpersonal forwardness a more normal part of your life.

Ensure that your environment is wired to produce an amount of randomness. Most workplaces attempt to overly control conflicts. They might simply repress them by implying that "rocking the boat" is not welcome, or by sending every disagreement to HR. More often than not, most workplaces simply neglect, avoid, and paper-over conflict. These workplace cultures and leaders value superficial peace over truth and honesty. Other organizations ensure that all conflicts are squeezed into impersonal grievance procedures that do little to help the relationship of those involved and often make the conflict between them worse by focusing on official sanctions and punishment.

Instead, encourage colleagues to address conflict more informally and organically *as it happens*. Reward and compliment courageous risk-taking. Thank people for bringing concerns to you directly. Insist that coworkers talk to one another directly, not through intermediaries, and certainly not via gossip and innuendo.

Accept that you cannot control the behavioral choices of others. Conflict is often avoided due to fear that the outcome will not be predictable. Here's the rub: the choices of others are never entirely predictable. Accept it.

All that any of us can really control is our own behavior and the process by which we engage others. Building those explicit behavioral habits and engagement skills is the entire point of this book. Once you are confident in your own skills and approach to interpersonal risk, how others choose to react is really not that important. They will do what they will do. You can handle it. The world won't end.

Taking regular daily risks, encouraging colleagues to address conflict directly in the moment, and accepting that all we can really control is our own behavior are the keys to going beyond resilience. These three factors will help you become a leader who thrives and strengthens in the face of conflict. You will become antifragile only when you embrace the suck.

TOXIC WORKPLACE BEHAVIOR PROFILE

THE PEACEMONGER

Code Name: The Peacemonger
Motto: I'm great. How are you?
Favorite Song: "Everything Is Awesome" by Tegan and Sara
Favorite Movie: Anything animated, preferably by Pixar
Behavior: Can't we all just get along?

No, Peacemonger, we can't.

Yes, we know that all this office tension makes you feel uncomfortable. It makes all of us uncomfortable too. That's why we need to deal with it.

In the section "Stay in the Problem," I discussed the dangers of resolving conflicts too soon. We humans don't like uncertainty. And conflict brings big-time uncertainty. For some of us, the drive to control the fear of uncertainty in relationships can develop into a compulsion. It can turn you into a Peacemonger.

The Peacemonger doesn't just *prefer* things to be peaceful. They deeply *need* things to be peaceful—even if that means squashing, denying, or contriving superficial resolution to conflicts. This fear of conflict usually manifests as either avoidance or control-oriented behaviors.

The avoidant Peacemonger tends to minimize conflict and squash negative feelings in themselves and others. This is the person who papers-over disagreements and minimizes hurts. They frequently table tough discussions for another day and another meeting that never seems to happen.

As a supervisor, they will go to great lengths to avoid open and real discussion of thorny issues. They will shift staff to other departments, alter who supervises whom, move desks—anything that will stave off the interpersonal confrontations that they fear. This can waste a tremendous amount of time, attention, and resources. Relational conflicts are hardwired to come to the surface. It takes a lot of energy, and even creativity, to persistently push issues and feelings back underground in a team. This mix of hypervigilance and conflict avoidance is exhausting and a leading cause of leadership burnout.

The longer conflicts are avoided and minimized, the more likely it will be that workplace relationships unravel in ways that are unpredictable, emotionally magnified, and chaotic (i.e., all hell breaks loose).

The control-orientated Peacemonger is the mirror image of the avoidant variety, but the results are the same. This person loves to be the first on the scene during a conflict—so that they can take over, control the problem, and make it go away. An avoidant Peacemonger might even pair up with a control-oriented Peacemonger. Frequently, a senior leader who habitually seeks to avoid conflict will use another leader or staff member to intervene, control, and make problems go away.

They develop a symbiotic relationship and might even believe that they excel at handling conflict, when in reality they are just pushing it away.

Sometimes this type of dysfunction can take over whole HR departments. Instead of leading others to proactively address the roots of conflict, the department becomes the conflict suppressor for avoidant leadership—keeping a lid on things and kicking the conflict can down the road.

Control-oriented Peacemongers will often use the outer forms and buzzwords of healthy conflict engagement but will use them to suppress rather than explore the conflict. Conversations will orient around the Peacemonger's feelings and needs instead of those of the actual direct stakeholders in the conflict.

For instance, the Peacemonger might invite others to "have a conversation and share our feelings about what happened," when what this actually means is: "Let me tell you why this all needs to stop because it's making me uncomfortable and that's not OK here."

Do Not: When trying to shift the behavior of a Peacemonger, remember that this person is rarely seeking to harm anyone. They are simply experiencing a more extreme form of the discomfort and fear that we all have regarding conflict.

Unlike the Submarine or the Brutus, this person is actually trying to help. They are just habitually "helping" in a way that ultimately makes things worse, which is truly not what they intend.

As such, avoid using an overly adversarial approach or blaming language.

Do: Acknowledge the positives. The Peacemonger recognizes that there is a problem (that's great!) and is trying to do something about it (also great!). Make sure that they hear this from you.

Reinforce that you both want the same outcome—happy, healthy coworkers with strong, positive relationships.

Then you need to help them talk about their personal feelings and fears. Most people originally became Peacemongers for understandable reasons. If you can build enough trust, give them the space to talk about their personal stories around conflict.

For instance, if they grew up in a house with lots of sudden explosive anger, maybe generally keeping a lid on things and being avoidant wasn't such a bad idea as a child. It might have helped them survive— emotionally and physically.

Or, if they've had a long relationship with a self-medicating addict, or have had addiction issues themselves, perhaps they learned to rely on pain avoidance as a primary coping strategy. If so, leading conflict principles such as "embrace the suck" are going to be a long, hard sell.

If they grew up around neglectful or disconnected caregivers, they simply might not have seen much role-modeling around conflict—because no one really cared enough to fight. And any conflict that did arise, however small, felt like an existential threat to an already tenuous relationship. Or maybe they were just raised in an environment that pressured them to be "nice" all the time.

All of the above examples are common stories from my work helping leaders change their peacemongering ways. Universally, encourage your local Peacemonger to:

- **Speak about their own feelings and in the first person.** Don't let them speak for others. Ask them to speak for themselves. Don't let them avoid taking personal risks by hiding in third-person language (i.e., It's not, "We are upset" or "The organization is concerned." Instead, it's, "I am upset" and "I am concerned.").
- **Process their own personal stories around conflict.** See above.
- **Experience real and meaningful conflict engagement—repeatedly and over time.** You will need to show

the Peacemonger how to have the conversations and confrontations they have been avoiding. They need to see that their fear of conflict is wildly disproportional to the actual risks. You need to show them how it's done, perhaps many times. Don't underestimate how long this will take. A year or more of repeated practice and exposure would not be uncommon. Gradually help them to take more and more responsibility for leading these interactions on their own as they overcome their fears.

ROUND TWO:
FACING OURSELVES

OVERVIEW

I have good news. You need far less than you think to make a fundamental change: personally, professionally, or organizationally. The tough news is that making a firm decision to change is hard. In fact, it's the hardest part of any transformation process.

Very few leaders have had the life experience or the mentorship to learn how to do this strategically, deliberately, and on demand when circumstances require it. Most of us do not confidently sail into the future—at least not in all areas of life. We are dragged into it. If you're like me, we often go kicking and screaming. Yet, making firm decisions is one of the key abilities that separates a good-enough leader from a great one.

You can't buy resolve from a consultant. There's no packaged program of defined steps that will download determination into your psyche. When it's time to change, you either will or you won't. It's entirely in your hands. Like Yoda said, "Do or do not. There is no try."

What the master from Dagoba meant with his advice is that you must decisively put yourself into a position where you will either succeed in making the change or fail boldly. To "try" is to hedge your bets, or rather, your ego. To "try" is to leave yourself an out. It's an attempt to bet on yourself while wagering as little as possible. It's the mental equivalent of hoisting the sail, casting off your mooring ropes, putting one foot on the boat, and leaving one foot on the dock. You won't be going anywhere except into the water.

Later in this book, we'll cover the final principle, Lead from the Future: Leading Conflict Principle 9. In this principle I'll discuss how to lead change in an organization by behaving as if the thing you want to be true has already happened. Then work backward to fill in the relational or cultural architecture that will cement that reality into place. In order to get there, we'll need the foundation of principles 1 through 8.

Remember, like boxing, first you learn how to stand, then how to move, then how to breathe, then how to punch, then how to duck, and only then how to fight. Round One covered foundational habits and mindsets: i.e., move toward things that scare you, practice doing the hard things, and embrace the fact that conflict and quality relationships entail some suffering and sacrifice.

The principles in Round Two will build on this by covering the habits and mindset needed to change your own behaviors and approach to relationships while others are watching. Because as a leader, others are always watching.

The central fallacy around which many coaching programs and leadership consultants build their process is that the order of change activities for an individual looks something like this:

Present → New Skill/Process/Program Acquisition → Change to Desired Future

Rationally, this is true. You start from the current reality, recognize a gap or needed skill, acquire new knowledge and training, and then deploy and integrate that skill to create a new pattern of behavior.

In reality, though, the psychology of change for the individual looks more like this (especially when there is significant risk or self-doubt involved):

Present → Change to Desired Future → New Skill/Process/Program Acquisition

This means that there's a definitive, though often overlooked, step that comes before the acquisition of new skills and abilities. This is the stage where a leader must make a definitive decision to step into the future before it is fully formed. This is not simply a trick of "mindset." It is the tangible and concrete ability to selectively and prudently say, "This is happening. Come what may." Then, back it up with action.

This is hard to teach, which is why most mentors don't "sell" it. It's the part that most clients want to avoid, often in the vain hope that they can outsource the risk, fear, and doubt related to change. However, proficiency in this stage of change can be taught. The first step is that leaders and organizations must face the potential barriers that make this stage of change hard. The premise of this book is that the best way to overcome these barriers is to face them head-on by proactively practicing a principle that is the barrier's mirror opposite.

The hardest part of leading conflict, and any martial art, is gaining greater mastery of, and understanding about, yourself. Like Muhammad Ali said, "My toughest opponent has always been me."

In Round One we covered:

- Fear of failure (Move toward Fear: Principle 1)
- Aversion to uncertainty (There's No Nice Way to Poke Someone in the Eye: Principle 2)
- Avoidance of suffering (Embrace the Suck: Principle 3)

In Round Two, we'll address:
- Feelings of "impostership" (Fake It until You Make It: Principle 4)
- Fear of exposure (Be Radically Transparent: Principle 5)
- Learning new skills while everyone is watching (Grow in Public: Principle 6)

If this early step is skipped, no new practice or program will stick. It's not the acquisition of new skills that changes your mindset. It's the change of mindset and determination to live differently that leads you to acquire the skills and competencies that eventually create a new lived reality.

Here's a short story that proves the point.

PRETENDER OR CONTENDER?

In my middle school years, my parents recognized our neighborhood outside of Northeast Philadelphia was deteriorating quickly. The occasional neighborhood scuffle was being replaced with serious violent crime. Working-class kids drinking some beers they stole from Dad's fridge in the garage was being supplanted by a growing hard-drug trade. It was time to go, so we moved to a very rural area an hour north of the city.

I attended a very small high school. In addition to our wonderful language programs, top-shelf quiz bowl team, and excellent theater program, we were also known for having perhaps the losing-est football team in the state. Since they first hit the field in the early 1970s, this team had precisely zero winning seasons by the time I joined. If memory serves, they often went several years without winning a single league game.

There were lots of excuses bandied about for this spectacularly consistent underperformance. The school was small. Soccer was a winning program that drew some of the best natural athletes away from gridiron greatness. Funding was limited. Etc., etc., etc.

However, it's one thing to be a mediocre sports program. It's quite another to be this consistently awful through multiple generations of players and coaches. Then, just around the time I moved into the school district, a new team of coaches correctly assessed what the real problem was. This history of failure had nothing inherently to do with the people in the program or its funding. The problem was the culture.

One coach in particular is remembered by all. He was a tough-as-nails combat veteran who had done multiple tours as a Marine in Vietnam. He had, as they say, "command presence." When he talked, you listened. He didn't need to yell. He just needed to look you in the eye.

At the time, we were the scraggliest bunch of unlikely candidates for transformation that you could imagine. We were (depending on your generational preference) the Dirty Dozen, the Bad News Bears, or dare I say, the Mighty Ducks.

Instead of practice one Monday afternoon, this coach called a team meeting. As usual, we had lost badly the previous Saturday. As we sat around goofing off and talking about everything except football, the coach walked in and simply stood at the front of the room, staring at us. We quieted down, but he didn't speak. He just stared and stared . . . and stared.

Eventually, he said with a strange mix of sadness and intensity, "You didn't just lose. Hard as losing is, that's something we can work on. No, you gave up. I saw it. You saw it. You gave up last Saturday and you've been giving up all year. This isn't just about football. It's about who you are and who you want to be in life." His eyes began to water. We had never seen him like this.

He said, "I can teach you everything you need to know about football, but I can't give you self-respect. That's something you have to give to yourself."

You could have heard a pin drop. Now, a few guys were also quietly tearing up. Coach continued with something I'll never forget:

"You need to decide if you're a pretender or a contender. If you're only here to pretend, to wear a jersey around school and date cheerleaders, we don't need you. I'll field a team of freshmen who want to win before I'll field a team of pretenders."

He told us plainly, "Pretenders never win. They don't deserve to win."

Heads hung low.

"Or are you contenders? Being a contender doesn't mean that you'll win every game. It does mean that you'll train to win. You'll run every play to win. You'll leave everything on the field at every game, every weekend.

It means you'll start doing the one thing I can't make you do: believe in yourselves."

He ended by saying, "There's no practice today. If you're not 100 percent committed, if you're just a pretender, leave your jersey in the room before you leave. We don't need you and I don't want you. I only want contenders at practice tomorrow, because we're going to start training like young men who intend to win."

Then he left us in the room not knowing what to do next. What followed was a lot of soul searching. New leaders spoke up. Promises were made. For a fifteen-year-old kid, it was the first time I was treated like a true adult. Like Coach said, this wasn't about football anymore. It was about what kind of men we wanted to be. It was the beginning of something new.

Those of us who showed up the next day should have also been told to "prepare for hell," as the coaches made good on their promise that a new day had dawned. The intensity of practice increased dramatically, to put it mildly.

Over the next year, we starting doing all the things that winning teams do. We started a yearlong training cycle, three-a-day practices in the summer, powerlifting programs, sprinting coaches, etc. We also showed up on time for practice. We stopped partying before games. All those things helped, but none of them alone or together were the reason for what became a miraculous turnaround.

We started acting like a winning team long before we actually were one. Many people mocked the change in behavior, and deservedly so based on our past performance. This upped the psychological ante and meant we had to make it real—every single Saturday. Coach had convinced us to put our self-respect on the line, to risk ridicule and public failure. We desperately wanted to earn the new identity we were now practicing. We weren't pretending anymore. After grinding it out like this for a year, the first game of the new season finally arrived.

This little high school not only had the worst football team in the league, we also had the most meager band. The few drums and squeaky, off-key horns were just as sad as our team's history. So, in our opening game of this new year, the band was benched. As the crowd waited for us to take the field, there was a long pause. The band stayed seated. Then, the opening chords of Guns N' Roses' Welcome to the Jungle blared at maximum volume from the field's speakers.

We had a few additional surprises in store for everyone that day. In recognition of our hard work in the off-season, the coaches had replaced our tattered and outdated '70s-era jerseys with some new ones that matched the type worn by Penn State at the time, a champion division-one team. The similarities would not be lost on the crowd or our opponents.

Also, our school mascot was the "Pirates." Right before the game, the coaches told us to tear the dorky buccaneer-style logos off our helmets and throw them in the garbage. Coach said, "You're a new team. You're new men and you deserve a new symbol." He then opened a box and passed out our new logo: a skull and crossbones. "This is your symbol now. Put that on your helmets."

He continued, "That team waiting out there thinks you're a joke. What they don't know is that you're now a team to be feared. And we're gonna show 'em." As we lined up at the locker room door and prepared to take the field, the coaches added another final touch. Four younger kids, little brothers of some of the teammates, showed up to march out in front of us. They carried long flagpoles and slowly unfurled gigantic black "Jolly Roger" skull-and-crossbones flags.

For a bunch of teenagers, many of us being truly tested for the first time in life, it was completely . . . badass. We emerged from the locker room and marched into battle as a team transformed. "Welcome to the jungle, baby!"

That day, we beat the previous year's league champs. "Aww, just a fluke . . . ," many said.

Then we beat the second-ranked team. With our newfound determination, we racked up a couple more wins before the end of the year. It was the best season in school history, but we still ended one game shy of a winning record. We stuck to it with even more determination in the off-season.

The next year, we hit the field even harder. We had the first homecoming game win in school history (yeah, really). We ended the season 6–5, decided by the final play of the final game, against the local rival. Pretty sweet.

Admittedly, "first winning season in school history" isn't the most glorious of distinctions. You don't get a trophy for that. Yet it wouldn't have been possible if we didn't decide we were going to be contenders, not pretenders. Compared to the past, we felt like champs. No one gave it to us or made it easy. There was nothing mystical about it. We started winning when we decided to behave like we deserved to win. Then we did the excruciatingly hard work to make it happen—not the other way around.

When he took the position, our coach realized that there was no path to success within the prevailing cultural reality. He, like us, was enmeshed in a story that would always be about losing, failure, and quitting. We were all playing parts handed down to us. The faces were different, but the story was always the same, year after year. Depressing as it was, that story was strong and durable. Coach didn't just change the story. He scrapped it and started a new one.

At first, he was the only person in that story. As he said, he was only going to coach contenders. He meant it and made good on that promise. Some seniors and juniors with bad attitudes were benched or sent packing after that locker room speech. In their place, he put fired-up freshmen and sophomores in the starting line-up when needed. I was fortunate to be one of them. Gradually, he and the rest of the coaches built a new future from scratch, brick by brick, person by person, practice by practice.

He taught me one of the greatest leadership lessons of my life. If you want to change the story of an organization (or yourself), you lead by being the first person to go all-in on the future. Coach was willing to risk failing miserably, and potentially look like a fool in the process, to help us create a different future.

In my day, the football field was a pot-holed mud puddle. The stands were tiny and usually quite empty—even when we started winning. We had no lights, so games were always on Saturday mornings. But not long ago, I drove past my old high school on a Friday night. Huge stadium lights glowed far into the sky and lit up the new professional-grade turf field. Hundreds of fans were packed into a new and expanded stadium paid for with huge donations from the community. They'd been a winning team for a while, and they had a stadium to match.

The guys on the field and people in the stands were living in a new story—one that started decades ago. It started when a coach walked into a musty room, looked a doubtful group of young men in the eye, and said:

The future is here. Who's coming?

PRINCIPLE 4:
FAKE IT UNTIL YOU MAKE IT

Everyone wants to be a hero.

This desire is deeply imprinted in our human hardwiring. In fact, throughout history we have told one primary story. It's the hero's story, and it goes something like this.

A person (usually young) is born in obscurity or in disadvantageous conditions (i.e., poverty, orphaned, broken relationships, etc.). They become aware of a great injustice, problem, or challenge that seems intractable. They sense, or otherwise learn, that they have great and hidden potential to make a difference in the world. They meet a guide who helps them develop this potential. They face obstacles and defeat the forces of evil or solve a great problem, while also resolving an internal dilemma. The hero then returns to something akin to "normal" life, but now transformed by hard-won experience, skill, and wisdom.

The hero's story can look quite different on the outside. Luke Skywalker, Mulan, Frodo Baggins, and Buffy the Vampire Slayer occupy very different worlds and might appear to have little in common. However, each of their stories follows the same basic pattern. Also, there is one primary experience shared by all heroes: they begin their quest feeling unprepared, ill-equipped, and unworthy.

Long before the hero slays the dragon, vanquishes the villain, or restores peace to the galaxy, they look in the mirror and say, "Who am I kidding? I can't do this." They feel like an imposter pretending to be something they are not. At this point, the guide helps them learn that heroes are not all-powerful. Instead, real heroes are those who feel unworthy but find the courage to go forward anyway. Only then does the hero discover their full potential.

This archetypal story is powerful because it captures the essence of learning and mastery—both in the micro context of developing new skills and in the macro context of a life well lived.

The mastery of new skills requires that you practice behaviors that do not feel natural. You will not feel like "yourself." You will feel awkward and unsteady. If the stakes are high and there are metaphorical dragons to slay, you will feel like a child with a sword that is too heavy and armor that doesn't fit.

But as every hero learns, you cannot wait until you feel truly ready. You will need to fake it until you make it. Consider the first three principles of leading conflict: Move toward Fear, There's No Nice Way to Poke Someone in the Eye, and Embrace the Suck. Those three principles give you the foundation you need to lead conflict with more confidence and strategic intention.

Don't wait to feel ready to use the skills discussed in this book. You know enough to begin the journey. You can only learn the rest of what you need to know along the way. A hero who begins their journey fully competent and prepared to meet all challenges is no hero. No one wants to read that story or see that movie, because success is expected and assumed. However, your story is fascinating. You have fears and doubts. You have the humility to question your readiness and the courage to consider your potential. In other words, you're a real person—just like the rest of us.

In the meantime, you will need to practice behaving as if you know what you are doing. As a leader you should be real, honest, and authentic. But paradoxically, there are occasions while leading conflict when you need to act as if you know exactly what to do—even though you are unsure. A friend's jiu-jitsu coach has another phrase for this phase of change: "face it until you make it." The hardest thing isn't a lack of skill. It's admitting to that lack. It's only when we face that reality that we are able to start advancing.

Consider Harvey Keitel's advice in the movie U-571 to a new submarine captain who admitted to his crew in the middle of combat that he really had no idea what to do next. As Harvey says, "The skipper always knows what to do—whether he does or not." Harvey wasn't telling the new skipper to lie. He was telling him that with command comes the occasional responsibility to keep your doubts to yourself to help others find the courage and confidence they need to act.

As you prepare to take action, and fake it (or face it) until you make it, remember these three truths:

1. You might not be an expert at leading conflict, but if you've been reading this book, you're probably more prepared than most of the other people in the room.
2. Decide and take action. The worst decision is no decision. Don't fail to act for fear of making a mistake.
3. Behave like the leader you wish you were. Eventually, you'll realize that you've become that person.

FIGHT TIP

ACTION CURES FEAR

As we covered earlier, fear causes paralysis, the tendency to freeze in the face of danger.

When faced with fear, it takes practice to decide and take action. The worst decision is no decision. Self-doubt is a response to fear, not its cause. It's how we give ourselves "permission" not to act in the face of fear, danger, and uncertainty. Don't fail to act for fear of making a mistake, failing, or looking foolish.

Here's the hardest part. When fear has taken over, you can't think your way out of it. The thinking part of your brain is not in control. You have to act your way out of it. Plus, if there is a real crisis at hand and your team is looking to you for answers, you can't wait until the fear passes. So, what do you do? The answer is easy to understand, but it takes lots of practice. Simply put:

Action cures fear.

Use this like a mantra. When you feel afraid, don't put off the conversation or whatever needs to be done. Don't schedule a meeting for next week. Don't give yourself an excuse, or put it on a list, or let it slide and hope the issue goes away. Take an action. It doesn't even matter if the action "works" or fixes anything. The point is to never be paralyzed. Nine times out of ten, the fear will evaporate when you act.

Our fears are almost always worse than the reality. The action puts you back in touch with the reality of the situation instead of what's going on in your head.

The more you do this, the more habitual it will become. This is what conquers the proverbial "fear of fear itself." When others hesitate, be the one who acts. Over time, fear will become something that's "just there," in the background or floating around the room.

You can recognize its presence but deny its ability to paralyze you. You do that by shortening the space and time between recognizing the fear and taking action.

"CUS" WORDS FOR WORK

OK. Here we are. Ready, like every young and inexperienced rookie from your favorite hero story, to set out on your journey. Once that first step is taken, everything after will be different. The natural question here, which will lead you to hold that foot up in the air, is: "Do I really want things to be different? After all, I'm used to the way things are in my relationships at work—maybe even at home. Is change really worth the cost? Am I ready?"

Some tasks are inherently unpleasant. No one likes rinsing out a garbage can after the bag has leaked. Few people enjoy scooping doggy-doo from the backyard, no matter how they love their furry friend.

Similarly, most of the tasks that surround workplace conflict are never going to be the tasks we look forward to or inherently enjoy, at least in the usual sense of the word. However, there are some things in life that simply need to be done. Developing the humility to do them regardless of our own fears, tastes, and preferences is the key to leading conflict.

This reminds me of a quote by legendary boxing trainer Constantine "Cus" D'Amato. Cus trained some of the greatest champions of the twentieth century, such as Floyd Patterson, José Torres, and "Iron" Mike Tyson. Reflecting on the contradictions inherent in purposely entering a ring where you know that you will experience danger and pain, Cus is reported to have said something like:

"You have to do what you hate, but do it like you love it."

As covered in Move toward Fear: Leading Conflict Principle 1, Cus encouraged his boxers to view fear like fire. Fire can rage out of control and destroy, or it can be used to create and do useful work. An eighteen-year-old kid who wants to be a champion has only two choices: Let that fear control you and run away. Or face it, master yourself, and make it work for you.

Psychologically, there's very little difference in our responses to physical and interpersonal danger. Our first and natural response is to avoid and run away—unless you've trained yourself to do otherwise. That is the hardest part of learning how to box or lead conflict. Skipping rope, practicing proper form, and getting up early to work out all pale in comparison to the bigger challenges, such as performing while under attack, relaxing while moving at full power, and working through the personal demons and weaknesses that every fighter fears the most.

Similarly, learning how to structure a supervision meeting or utilize a simple feedback method is relatively easy compared to developing the ability to actually use them under pressure in the face of uncertainty and intense negative emotions. Learning how to operate and make wise decisions while under psychological and emotional duress requires a simple set of skills that you've practice so frequently that you'll be able to deploy them under pressure without having to think much about it. There are no shortcuts. This takes time and repetition.

Conflict skills that require everyone to be in a calm and Zen-like state of reflection are useless in most real-life situations. Authentic human behavior is unpredictable and unscripted. Leaders should train and practice accordingly. A boxer doesn't see a punch and then think hard about ducking, rolling, and counterpunching. He just does it. This isn't because he was born with innate skill. He does it because he's practiced it so many times in similar situations that the behavior becomes automatic—overriding his natural fear and hesitancy.

FIGHT  TIP

BAYONET!

Here's a tip from one of my fighting heroes, General Joshua Lawrence Chamberlain. The Battle of Gettysburg (July 1863) is widely considered to be the definitive turning point of the US Civil War. Chamberlain's decisions that day changed the course of history.

Charged with holding a small hill (Little Round Top) on the extreme left flank of the Union lines, he and the soldiers of the Twentieth Maine Regiment faced wave after wave of assaults from elite Confederate units.

Chamberlain understood that if the position was overtaken, the Confederate army would likely win the day—and perhaps the war.

Each time, Chamberlain and his men repulsed a Confederate force of superior numbers and experience. And each time, the Twentieth Maine found themselves with fewer men and less ammunition to continue the fight.

Chamberlain eventually realized that the regiment could not withstand many more assaults. Many commanders would have ordered a retreat—attempting to save the lives of their men from an ultimately indefensible position.

Instead, Chamberlain give the historic order, "BAYONET!"

The men looked at one another with disbelief and then fiery determination. They fixed bayonets, steeled their courage, and charged down the hill toward the astonished Confederate units, who quickly surrendered. Later, even Confederate officers recalled this one decision as perhaps the single most courageous act they had ever seen in war.

The Union left flank held. The North prevailed at Gettysburg. The tide of the war was turned. A new era of US history had begun.

Sometimes, leading conflict comes down to a few key moments. Eventually, you will find yourself in an untenable position—understaffed, under resourced, and outgunned. Many times, the wisest thing to do is to retreat, reconsider, and reposition.

But there will come a time when the right thing to do will not be the safe thing to do. You will need to decide, like Chamberlain, whether you and your team are ready to fix bayonets.

FUNDAMENTALS WIN FIGHTS

Here's the next thing Cus would tell you: fundamentals win fights. Don't step into the ring for your first fight thinking about whose hand will be raised in the end. Go into the ring thinking about the fundamentals you've practiced. Work the fundamentals and the wins will come.

Think about the story I shared in the opening of this book—about the conflict experts who froze in the face of real conflict. They didn't habitually practice the fundamentals in their own work lives and relationships. So, they could not perform under pressure outside of the controlled environment of a training example or classroom case study.

To build on the analogy, just because someone knows how to throw a punch, duck, and shuffle their feet, that doesn't mean they know how to box. A real fighter knows how to do all those fundamentals simultaneously, instinctually, and on demand. For instance, a deep understanding of the neurology of trauma and conflict can be an incredibly important area of knowledge. Understanding how to craft a quality feedback statement is another important skill. The list goes on. However, if you tend to panic and hyperventilate when faced with an angry coworker, you need something more than a depth of scientific understanding or a "toolbox" full of useful individual practices.

The reality is that under intense psychological pressure in any endeavor, you're going to remember how to do only a few simple things. These will be the things that you have practiced so many times that you can perform them instinctually. Under stress, as the Greek poet Archilochus said, "We do not rise to the level of our expectations; we fall to the level of our training."

You learn how to play the piano by playing the piano. You learn how to play football by playing football. You learn how to box by actually boxing and sparring. And you can only learn how to lead conflict by actually leading it—not by avoiding, suppressing, or just reading about it.

FIGHT TIP

DO NOTHING

I know; I know. This sounds like a complete contradiction to the last two tips. Stick with me here.

In the fight tip *Stay in the Problem*, I encourage you to learn to love the mess when it comes to workplace conflict.

As I said in that section, it's best not to act until:

- The conversation includes those closest to the problem
- There is a shared understanding and definition of the problem itself
- All potential options for action are understood and digested by the group

Here's a secret. Sometimes doing nothing is the most strategic action of all. Avoidance isn't good. But that's different. When you avoid, you are trying to get away from a problem.

Purposely doing nothing means that you are choosing to slow things down, let things play out, or let others step up and act. This is, paradoxically, an action.

The difference is your intent and attention. When you strategically do nothing, the problem still has your full attention. You are simply choosing not to act on the situation personally—for now. Leaders like action. Leaders like to fix things. Leaders feel compelled to demonstrate their competency by making order from chaos—by cleaning up messes.

This also means that the biggest barrier to your team "staying in the problem" is most likely you. The next time you get a long email begging you to intervene, or your team tries to "delegate up" and send a problem to you for fixing, shake things up. Help them stay in the problem. Take action. Do nothing.

KIND IS MANDATORY—NICE IS OPTIONAL

Here's a short story about leaders in a new organization being asked to practice a new "identity" as leaders. I was recently invited to speak at a leadership retreat. The organization is based in a region of the country that is known for many things. They have great restaurants, excellent schools, and beautiful rolling countryside. They are also known for being very, very nice.

A place renowned for niceness is wonderful if you're a tourist. It's probably a great place to raise a family. It might even be a pleasant place to go to the DMV. However, if you're trying to introduce innovation and culture-change in an organization full of staff accustomed to being "nice" as a core part of their identity, this can actually be a problem.

At the retreat, we were covering There's No Nice Way to Poke Someone in the Eye: Leading Conflict Principle 2, and someone said:

> John, I get it and I agree. Dancing around hard conversations for fear of hurting someone's feelings doesn't help anyone. But I'm still struggling with how to put this into action with my staff. Everyone in my unit places such a premium on "being nice." I'm afraid that being more upfront and transparent will be portrayed as meanness. We do shy away from tensions and tend to avoid conflict, but it is a pleasant place to work most of the time. What should I do?

Excellent question. Here's one way to answer it: Stop focusing on being nice. Instead, insist on practicing kindness. Niceness is the desire to produce a subjective feeling of emotional pleasure in others. This isn't necessarily a bad thing. However, the desire to be seen as nice has more to do with our own needs than the needs of those around us. It feels good to be nice. It's a positive experience that rewards us with dopamine and decreased relational risk. However, compulsive niceness can also be deeply selfish.

Here's the contrast. Kindness is objectively oriented toward what is most likely to assist the person in front of us. True kindness is independent of the feelings it might produce in us or the other person.

Niceness is about what people want. Kindness is about what people need.

As a leader, giving people what they want or what they're asking for, or telling them what they want to hear, will indeed produce pleasure in the relationship. It might also be incredibly unkind. There's nothing kind about withholding feedback that might be the key to someone's growth. It's not kind to confirm others for behavior or thinking that is likely to harm them personally or professionally.

Genuine kindness requires risk and, often, confrontation. It requires leaders who are willing to set aside the self-gratifying desire to be seen as nice and occasionally sacrifice relational peace in order to seek a higher good in the people they serve.

Also, leaders who habitually insist on being "the nice one" typically leave a lot of interpersonal heavy lifting for others to do, either now or in the future. That tough conversation avoided today will become someone else's crisis tomorrow. If you have an organizational culture that overvalues niceness, consider how this might be limiting innovation, relationships, and learning. Often, the most important conversations are the ones that people aren't allowed to have.

It's great to work with many nice and pleasant people. However, growth requires something deeper and riskier. It requires an intensive commitment to genuine kindness and leaders willing to do the hard and needed thing, not the nice thing.

TOXIC WORKPLACE BEHAVIOR PROFILE

THE DIVA

Code Name: The Diva

Motto: Enough about me, let's talk more about me.

Favorite Song: "Shiny" by Jemaine Clement as Tamatoa the Crab in Disney's Moana

Favorite Movie: *The Devil Wears Prada*

Behavior: Oh, Diva . . . if the world only recognized how awesome and fabulous you are. Always. Everyday. Right now. You're brilliant. You're charming. You know just what to say and how to say it. You just don't know when to stop.

The Diva is the unhealthy extreme of faking it until you make it. They fake it without making it, until eventually the idea of who they are outstrips the reality, which never catches up.

We typically have a love/hate relationship with the Divas in our life. Like Tamatoa the Crab in Disney's Moana, they are, in a word, shiny. And we like shiny things.

Frequently, the Diva is shiny because they have skills and talents that legitimately warrant praise and attention. However, the Diva uses those skills to garner ever more praise and attention—not to serve others. This is what sets the Diva apart from your run-of-the-mill attention hog or bore.

The Diva doesn't just like attention. The Diva needs and craves the attention of the team. The more the better. Their self-worth is dependent on it.

Think of Hollywood. This industry contains some amazing artists. It is also the highest concentration of attention-addicts in the world. The addiction to endless streams of attention even leads some to hope that, because they are good at one thing, perhaps they can be good at everything!

Case Study 1: Sean Penn's attempts at artsy novel writing. Yikes! Love your acting, but Faulkner you are not, my son.

Case Study 2: Sylvester Stallone's foray into modernist painting. Yo Adrian, I did it! (But shouldn't have.)

The possible exception to these artistic abominations is, of course, David Hasselhoff—or as his friends call him, "The Hoff." After four monumental seasons as the method-acting phenomenon behind the TV show Knight Rider, he also managed to briefly become a chart-topping pop singer in Germany. Well played, Hoff. Well played.

As we can see from Sean, Sylvester, and even the Hoff, the Diva doesn't know their limits, when to quit, or how to turn it off. Divas in the workplace drain creative energy from the team and misuse their real talents for selfish ends.

While they frequently garner admiration, they also breed passivity and dependence as teams become more focused on meeting the Diva's need for praise and attention rather than achieving results.

The good news is that this behavior is also draining for the Diva. It is an enormous amount of work to keep the spotlight on oneself at all times. Even if unconsciously, they spend more time than you can possibly imagine planning and engineering their next attention fix. They also live in fear of the day when the bright lights will shut off.

Do Not: Don't publicly shame the Diva on purpose. I know you want to. You fantasize about it. You dream about it. The Diva is just so full of themselves. If you could just cut them down to size in the next meeting . . .

But this will go badly. Go snatch a bottle from the hand of a committed drunk mid-swig. See what happens. Not pretty.

Attention is the Diva's drug. Forcibly tear it away from them and they will lash out. Intensely. And that's not particularly helpful to anyone.

Do: That being said, you should confront their behavior. Do so privately or in a small group at first.

This conversation should be planned and strategic. It's not typically fruitful to have these exchanges on the spur of the moment. You want this discussion to happen when the Diva is not performing or in the spotlight.

Ask pointed questions that encourage strategic reflection without passing blanket judgments.

For instance, say something like:

"I noticed that you did most of the talking in the last meeting. What is that like for you? Did you think about pausing for questions, or so others could contribute? What stopped you? What were you thinking about at the time? How could you make more space for other people in your meetings?"

To be fair to the Diva, much of their attention-seeking behavior is habitual and instinctive. Interrupt that cycle by suggesting specific actions that they can intentionally plan to carry out with others.

Don't let the Diva act on instinct. Make sure they develop and follow a plan to share the spotlight. In particular, the Diva needs to practice giving, listening, and publicly appreciating the contributions of others.

Help the Diva by substituting occasional, legitimate, and deeply meaningful feedback for the shallow stream of constant attention to which they've become accustomed. Tell the Diva that you value their real talents. Be specific. This praise is deserved and should not be withheld out of spite. Also, schedule regular short meetings with the Diva to see how the above is going—and praise them for honest efforts.

Humility check: We all crave attention and the admiration of peers on some level. If you are honest, you can likely relate to some of the Diva's behavior. After all, Divas are over-represented in leadership positions. Role model the behavior you expect from others by establishing some accountability with a trusted colleague or supervisor. Make some plans with them as discussed above. Admit it and talk about it. You might even *be* the office Diva. Process it with your team. Seriously, if you're the Diva, it's not like it's a secret. Try this:

- At the next team meeting, after you introduce the topic, schedule at least fifteen minutes of brainstorming and sharing—and do not speak. Tell the group you will just be listening.
- Even better: At the next team meeting, ask another team member to introduce the topic and another to close the meeting. Tell the group you will just be listening.
- Don't open or close a meeting for the next week. Help prepare other team members to do this.
- Give advice to three colleagues this week without talking about yourself in the process (harder than it sounds).

Over time, you will make more quality space for other people on your team to shine.

PRINCIPLE 5:
BE RADICALLY TRANSPARENT

It was 2008. The Great Recession was in full swing. An organization that was growing steadily until that point had nearly ground to a halt. It was very eerie in the office. The rush and crush of a once-busy international professional development and coaching business was gone. The phones were not ringing, and the usual flood of emails had slowed to a trickle. The last of our multiyear contracts were coming to an end. Event registrations were low.

We had recently launched a new and innovative graduate program after investing nearly a decade of sweat equity and what little surplus we could pool from our consortium of organizations. After a promising initial growth period following program launch, new student inquiries were way down. The rapid and unexpected loss of steady revenue from these programs was, in a word, crippling. I was nearly ready to grab my sandwich board and become a street corner preacher. Repent! The end is near!

For the first time in our thirty-year history, we were headed toward layoffs. We held a meeting with several hundred staff members to discuss the state of the organization and our plans to right the ship. The leadership spoke frankly about the current state of the business. We gave a detailed presentation of the finances and how the recession had created a perfect storm that we had not foreseen.

Several crucial revenue streams, key to the success of our business plan, had collapsed and were not likely to return. In order to survive, the organization would need radical restructuring and a new vision for its programs. Before continuing, we opened the floor for comments from anyone who would like to speak. Then, the unimaginable happened. Someone decided to say what they were really thinking. The staff member who politely took the mic was new. He had worked with us for about a year, in an entry-level position.

He said with great poise, "Thanks for sharing all this information and being so honest about the situation, but I do have a question. Everyone on the leadership team has said that this situation is unprecedented in your careers—that you've never had to lead an organization through a situation this dire."

The staff member continued politely, but directly, "Have you considered that maybe you're not the right leaders to see us through this? Maybe we need new leaders who have more experience in a business crisis like this one."

The room was quiet. I wasn't sure what to say. The honest truth was that this was the very question keeping me and many others up at night. I felt naked, exposed, disarmed.

The president at the time, our founder and my predecessor, paused with mic in hand. Then he taught me one of the most impactful lessons of my career. When in doubt, just say what you are really thinking. Be radically transparent.

He said, "Well, that's a really good question. I've been asking myself the same thing. Am I and the rest of the leadership capable of seeing us through this crisis? I guess the honest answer is that I don't know, but we are going to find out."

The president went on to talk about the origins of the organization and how he and a small group of collaborators had built it from the ground up. There had been other crises in our past, and each time we had collectively found a path through the adversity.

He concluded, "If you're asking for guarantees, I can't give them to you. All I can say is that we have a history of meeting challenges, and we are going to do our best. Also, the leadership can't do this alone. We need the help of all of the staff. We need your help and suggestions too. That's what the rest of this meeting is about. Thanks for taking a risk and being honest."

Radical transparency, in this conversation and many that followed, saved the organization.

The reality is that many of us were, mentally and emotionally, hanging on by a thread. If leadership had turned on the staff and been combative or defensive, our culture would have begun to unravel. Many would have started looking for an exit.

Our president's personal transparency said that it was OK to have doubts, to be afraid, and to just be tired—as many of us were. His response also said that we should not underestimate ourselves. If the past was the best predictor of future performance, then we should take heart.

Whenever the chips were down in the past, we had always pulled through. We made it through the Great Recession too. It was our shared commitment to radical transparency that gave us the courage to face the reality of the marketplace, our insecurities, and scariest of all, our potential.

Radical transparency when leading conflict doesn't mean saying whatever pops into your head or being ruled by emotion. It would have been too easy to lash out at that staff member. After all, he had been with us less than a year and here he was criticizing a founder and other leaders who had decades of experience running complex organizations.

Radical transparency means being real, but more than that, it means being humble.

The reality was that all of us were questioning our competence. Why didn't we see this coming? Why hadn't we acted sooner? Could we have forestalled the damage?

Sure, we could have hidden our doubts and given superficial and puffed-up reassurances to the staff. However, no one would have really bought it. They would have left wondering what else we were hiding or not telling them. Instead, everyone left that day with a deeper dedication to the leaders of our organization, who respected them enough to tell them the truth—not only about the organization but also about themselves.

Before we left, I turned to one of our directors and pointed at the new staff member who had challenged us. I said quietly, "What's that guy's name? He has a future here."

FIGHT TIP

DEPLOY WATERCOOLER COUNTERMEASURES

Here's a tip related to being radically transparent that is particularly helpful when contending with toxic behavior among colleagues.

In the Round One, Toxic Workplace Behavior Profile: The Submarine, we covered the stealthy threat posed by the office "submarine." The submarine will use informal settings (watercooler, parking lot, texts, etc.) as opportunities to criticize ideas, plans, coworkers, and leaders through gossip and innuendo. So, if approached by a submarine who attempts toxic conversation in an informal setting, how do you handle it? Here's an easy-to-remember watercooler countermeasure for waging effective antisubmarine warfare.

When the submarine shares a gossipy criticism or complaint with you about someone else, leadership, or a larger organizational issue, use a version of one of the following statements:

"I hear that you are upset about this. You really need to share it directly with [*insert name of person under discussion*]."

Or

"I hear that you are upset about this. You really need to share this with the person who can do something about it / the one who makes those decisions."

That's it. Don't engage further. You heard them. You made a healthy suggestion. Now you're done with this conversation.

Walk away and enjoy the rest of your day.

Be mind-numbingly consistent with responses like this every time you are approached. Eventually, they will stop trying to engage you in toxic conversation.

THE ART OF FOLLOWING

That was a story about a great boss, which begs a common question from clients, How do you follow a "bad" boss? The answer is: the same way you follow a good one.

Great leaders are only made from the ranks of great followers. Striving to be radically transparent is not a call to say any darn thing on your mind anytime you're thinking it or to stick it to the man as your everyday meeting strategy. Speaking truth to power can certainly be a good thing. The question is how to do that and have those in power actually hear it—maybe even like it. You do that by knowing what it means to "follow well" and the role that transparency plays in the leader/follower relationship.

By "followers" I don't mean passive doormats or sycophants. Those people are not effective followers, and they are not likely to become impactful leaders. There's an art to following. Especially if you aspire to be a valued leader, it's an art you must learn. Here are three laws of quality "following" that develop the skills and virtues necessary to produce exceptional leaders. Each law accomplishes a dual purpose.

These laws are a simple and concrete way to practice humility. The number one reason leaders fail is a lack of humility. In this context, humility means embracing your place in the organizational scheme of things and performing the duties of your position to the best of your abilities. The best leaders were also great dishwashers, parking lot attendants, and mail room workers at other points in their lives.

The nature of the work doesn't matter. You will do big things the way you do small things. Bring your best self to your job, whatever it may be. There's nothing magical that happens when you are bestowed with a position of great responsibility. An impressive title will not suddenly make you an impressive leader or a different person. How you perform your current duties will be how you perform your future duties.

There are people in your organization whose job it is to identify future leaders. This is what they are looking for, and paying attention to, in staff. Also, the laws are a way to lead from below.

As I've said many times, leadership has little to do with your title. Titles bestow more formal power, managerial and supervisory responsibility. Leadership exists in a related, but adjacent, domain. It's a relational field of action that operates beyond the firm black lines on the org chart. Titles won't tell you who all the leaders are in an organization. Behavior will.

The laws that follow apply regardless of whether you respect your boss or not. They apply whether your boss is a top-shelf superstar or a bumbling palooka. It doesn't matter if you work for St. Francis or Vlad the Impaler. Follow these laws because they are the right thing to do, not because you judge your boss to be worthy.

The "worthiness" of your supervisor has literally nothing to do with it. Don't let a bad boss turn you into a bad employee. If you work for a "Vlad," it might gall you that he or she will benefit in the short term from your honorable followership. However, these laws are ultimately aimed at your long-term good, not only theirs. Take the long view.

The three laws are:

1. Make them look good. No one values staff who actively undermine their supervisor, even if that supervisor is a jerk. Gossip, complaining, or throwing other leaders under the bus provides zero value to the rest of the organization. It's selfish and accomplishes nothing positive.

You make yourself look good (to the right people) by making those you serve look good. Don't lie for them, perpetuate fictions, or do anything unethical. However, do your level best to be the bright spot in your unit and help that team succeed. Fill the gaps, do what needs to be done, and help keep the ship afloat. Compliment your boss publicly about anything that is real and true.

Even though it stings, allow your boss to share in the credit when things go well, even if they had little to do with the success. Trust that other quality leaders in the organization will recognize who really did the work. Concrete external rewards might be long in coming, but eventually they will, assuming you are consistent and committed.

2. Decrease their stress. Deep down, even the most ego-deluded and horrible bosses know they are struggling. This produces tremendous internal stress and anxiety. This inner turmoil creates a vicious cycle of bad decisions and toxic behavior. Purposely amping up their stress by neglecting your own duties or secretly working at cross-purposes to them only feeds this cycle. No one wins in that scenario.

Especially if your boss is a true hot mess, the more you effectively support their ability to hold it together, the better life will be for everyone—especially you. Make sure they are ready for the big meeting. Remind them about the upcoming report deadline. Help them organize their maelstrom of dysfunction, to the extent that those things fall within your realm of responsibility.

3. Tell them the truth. Be supportive. Be caring. Be humble. But never, ever, lie for them or to them. Don't keep their secrets. Hold your tongue when necessary. But when you speak, tell them the truth. Always. To the greatest extent possible, support them in public and challenge them in private. Be honest, transparent, and if needed, blunt.

If they are making a mistake, tell them. If they are about to embarrass themselves, say so. It's not your job to rescue them from their own dysfunction. However, letting someone walk off a cliff without warning them is never the right thing to do. Be the honorable helper you would want if you were in their shoes, whether you think this particular person deserves it or not.

Finally, people get promoted for all sorts of reasons, most of which are probably out of your control. Those decisions might have been made before you showed up. Assuming you didn't make that decision, opining over why this person was ever given their position is neither productive nor particularly important to your immediate situation.

You took the job. You have the responsibility to serve the organization as best you can. When it's your time to lead, do better. This is the honest kind of "faking it until you make it." Whatever you're doing right now is your opportunity to practice and audition for the next big part you want to play in the drama of life. Criticizing the current leader won't make you ready.

The reality is that most bad bosses were also terrible followers. Practicing the art of following will help to ensure that when you get to sit in the big chair and be the boss, you'll be one of the great ones.

FIGHT TIP

BE A FLASHLIGHT

Similarly, consider the Brutus, workplace backstabber from Round One.

The Brutus uses trust and intimacy as a weapon. But they rarely do their work alone. Just like the historical Brutus, they will seek collaborators. What do you do if approached by a Brutus, not as a target but as a potential accomplice?

In short, be a "flashlight." Be radically transparent and shine a light on their behavior.

Silence and inaction are collusion. Remember, a real Brutus behaves this way habitually. You might not be the target now, but you could be in the future. If the Brutus is willing to violate another colleague's trust, they will be just as willing to violate yours at some point.

Tell the Brutus that you know what they are doing and that it is not OK. Tell them you will not participate.

If you have no provable facts, that's all right. It can be very effective to say something like, "I don't really know what's going on here. This doesn't feel good or right to me. I don't want to be a part of it."

You don't need prove anything. Just tell the person how the situation feels to you. They can take it or leave it. Even if the person is not up to anything icky or sneaky, it will be good for them to know that their actions are giving others that impression.

If the Brutus's actions are serious, consider going directly to the person they are targeting with the information. You can then decide what to do next, either together or with the team.

We all hope others would do that for us.

Also, if the Brutus is going to break this pattern of behavior, it will require people like you who are willing step up and take some risks. Do a solid for your teammates—and the Brutus. Be a flashlight.

FIGHT TIP

NEVER USE EMAIL

When you need to confront someone, the approach can make all the difference.

Always meet with the person face-to-face if possible. It's scarier at first but much more emotionally satisfying and likely to go well if you stand toe to toe. Most communication is nonverbal. You'll get a much better read on what the other person is really feeling if you are both in the same room. Plus, people are more likely to be reasonable in person than at a distance. Go the extra mile and show up in person. They'll know you're serious and that you care about the relationship.

Sometimes meet via video conference or phone. Understandably, today's post-pandemic, dispersed digital workforce and incredible videoconferencing technology make this "sometimes" mode of communication more necessary. Go for video over phone if it's available—even if you have to insist.

Never, and I mean never, confront someone (or a group) via text, social media, or email. No exceptions. All digital text formats are entirely tone-deaf to emotion. Actually, the receivers are likely to "hear" the worst possible tone in your writing. These media options are all cheap and easy confrontation cop-outs that create more problems than they solve. You can use email or other text mediums to set the meeting but not for delivering the content. You cannot lead conflict from a keyboard.

Be exceptional. Be a fearless confrontation champ. Walk down the hall and knock on the door or get that Zoom meeting on the books.

BE AN ALIEN ANTHROPOLOGIST

People are different. We each bring our own stories, assumptions, and world-view to work with us. Sometimes, you have a clear understanding of the ways in which you see and experience the world differently than your coworkers and how this plays out in behavior.

At other times, the behavior of those with whom you work can be simply perplexing. It's like you are from different planets. And in some sense, you are. When something about another person's behavior is alien to us, the impulse is usually to judge and reject that behavior. We all judge. It's unavoidable. Frequently, it's even useful.

However, radical transparency requires not just a personal commitment to trust and openness but also a disciplined appreciation for varied perspectives and life-stories of others. The greater the transparency in a workplace relationship or organizational culture, the more each contributor will be likely to know the important bits about each other's "story." Being an expert story finder and learner will not only help you be more transparent but will also help your team members to do the same.

Everyone is tasked with making thousands of decisions each day based on partial data and split-second impressions. We sort this information by making lots of small judgments based on our expectations of the world around us. Some of this is conscious, but most of this activity is subconscious and instinctual.

When the world doesn't behave the way we expect, we tend to reject what doesn't fit.

Many workplace conflicts are more about these mismatched expectations than they are about actual concrete disagreements. These "fights" typically revolve around radically different interpretations of a shared experience or event. Those differing interpretations are rooted in the diversity of life experiences and beliefs among colleagues.

When this happens, hold back on the judgment. Instead, become an alien anthropologist.

Try approaching the situation as if you have landed on a strange and alien planet orbiting a far-away star. Assume that your usual assumptions will not apply. The beings here are different and have evolved according to a radically different set of needs, assumptions about life, and expectations.

When you meet a Gorn (scary reptilian humanoid first seen in the Star Trek episode "Arena" [1967]) at work, don't fight like Kirk. Investigate like Spock. As an alien anthropologist, you are not here to judge. Instead, be curious. Learn their ways and how they think. When leading conflict as an alien anthropologist, practice these radically transparent strategies:

Model curiosity by admitting that you are surprised by what is happening and you are interested in learning more about it. Unexpected behavior frequently leads to toxic gossip and backlash unless someone demonstrates how to have an open and productive discussion about what is happening. The natural tendency is to judge and reject the novel and unexpected. Avoid this by taking an explicit and public position of curiosity as a leader.

Make the time needed to expand the conversation and go deeper into what happened. Avoiding awkward and uncomfortable conversations only saves time in the short term. Few things are more valuable than an opportunity for your team to learn more about what makes their colleagues tick. There are no shortcuts to really understanding one another. Seize each opportunity with discipline and focus.

Ask open-ended questions that encourage people to share their personal perspective, rather than making judgments or telling others what they should be thinking and feeling. Ask that people speak only for themselves. Some useful questions are:

- What were you thinking about at the time?
- What's been the hardest thing for you?
- What's the main issue for you in this conversation?
- What's one way you are contributing to the current situation?
- What would better look like for you?
- What's one thing you are willing to change about your own behavior or contribute to find a way forward?

Encourage storytelling. Most behavior at work has some analog in life outside the office. As you build trust within a team, encourage people to reflect on how similar behavior and events manifest in their relationships with friends and loved ones. When someone does something unexpected at the office, it's often a misapplication of a behavior that "works" in another area of life. These habits can be hard to change and it's useful to talk about that. A good leading question is: "Has this come up for you in other areas of life? Can you tell us more about that?"

Practice these strategies, and you'll set out into the cosmos with renewed confidence that your next alien encounter will be a fruitful learning experience instead of a clash of civilizations.

FIGHT TIP

DELETE THE QUESTION MARK

I guess what I'm saying is don't end a statement with a question mark?
Or...
When making a statement of fact, do not end it with a question mark.
Which statement above is clearer, more compelling, and more challenging to you?

The task of leaders is to give people what they need, not what they want. This requires you to project confidence. Confident and compassionate challenge is the essence of true kindness. In that effort, the small things really matter.

The habitual use of up-inflected question mark tones at the end of statements conveys doubt and weakness. It's the equivalent of saying, "you know . . . or not . . . whatever . . ." at the end of your sentence. It's often the subconscious attempt to "soften the blow," make what we are saying feel less confrontational, or maybe make us feel like less of a jerk. The problem is:

The implied question mark gives the audience permission to dismiss and resist something they often don't want to hear in the first place.

There is a time to inquire and a time to declare. Don't muddle the two. We invented the period for a reason. It's the best way to make a point. Use it.

WHEN TO DROP THE BIG ONE

A commitment to transparency means that you'll eventually find yourself in front of a big red button. You'll find yourself compelled to say the one thing that's true but not supposed to be said, the thing that is always avoided, the secret that everyone knows but pretends doesn't exist, or the critical piece of information that will vaporize the ways things are now.

When in doubt about whether to share what's on your mind or engage a tough situation, its usually best to lean toward taking the risk—take action, fix bayonets, and move toward fear. After all, it's the many small, mundane interactions of each day that provide us with most of the opportunities to build better relationships with colleagues and push a team toward more candor and transparency.

However, there are some opportunities that you should indeed approach with more thoughtful care and consideration. Some conflicts are like firecrackers. They make a big sound but aren't really that risky in the grand scheme of things. Other conflicts really are potential neutron bombs—things that will undoubtedly send massive shockwaves through a relationship or organization.

I'm occasionally asked the hard questions: How do you know if, and when, you should drop "the big one"? How do you know that it's time to say the thing that will be hugely disruptive, which, perhaps, no one wants to hear?

There are no hard-and-fast rules. Each situation is unique. You ultimately need to make your own decisions. But here are four criteria that I've used and recommended throughout the years to know when it might be time to press the big red button.

1. Is it true?

I don't mean that it feels true to you. I mean, is it literally and demonstrably true? Do you truly know that the facts you are about to lay out are correct?

We all have our own emotional and subjective reactions to certain experiences and situations. What might be a big deal to one person might not be experienced that way by another. While these types of events are certainly worth discussing, they usually revolve around misunderstandings and unintentional harm due to thoughtlessness or ignorance.

If you are going to potentially permanently alter a relationship, individually or with a team, by saying that thing that can't be unsaid, be sure that you have the unassailable facts of the situation and not just a hunch or impression.

Everyone is occasionally prone to undue suspicion, fear, and fragility in relationships. This can skew our judgment of people and situations. Before you take the biggest actions, be sure you have your own "crazy" in check.

I've been an organizational consultant and leadership coach for more than twenty years. I have a master's degree in counseling and a PhD in adult learning and change. And you know what? My first impressions and assessments of a situation are sometimes completely wrong. Give yourself plenty of time to process and confirm your conclusions before moving on to the next question.

2. Does it need to be said?

Just because something is true, doesn't mean it needs to be said out loud. We all notice lots of things about others with whom we work. Maybe you have some formal psychology training. Maybe you have great street-smarts and are excellent at figuring out what makes other people tick. Perhaps you are a highly advanced human lie detector. So what? Just because you've noticed something about a person, doesn't necessarily mean you need to verbalize it.

Judicious candor is refreshing in a relationship. Compulsively sharing everything you might happen to notice about someone is annoying. It can also be a form of passive-aggressive bullying if left unchecked. Before you speak, be sure that what you are sharing is for everyone's benefit and not only yours. If you're a leader, put the needs of others above your own.

3. Does it need to be said *by* me?

All right, now we're getting closer to "bombs away." However, even if it's true and you're convinced it needs to be said, that doesn't necessarily mean it needs to be said by you.

Maybe the issue that's gnawing at you is far outside your realm of responsibility. Maybe you lack key pieces of information to which others might have access. If so, unless it's a foundational ethical, safety, or legal concern, it might be wise to stay out of it. Some things are truly not your problem. Other things are (thankfully) none of your business.

Before you hit the "go" button, be sure that the issue at hand is fully within your professional charge. If it is, then you might have a responsibility to act. If not, it might be more appropriate to poke the person who's really supposed to be doing something about it.

4. Does it need to be said *now*?

OK. It's true, needs to be said, and you're the one who has a responsibility to say it. The last question is whether this is the right time and place. Truth has power. It should be delivered like a medicine, not wielded like a weapon.

No one likes a grandstander. The urge to "get it all out there" should be secondary to choosing the time and place likely to make the most positive impact possible. For instance, someone once knowingly called me at a cousin's funeral to confront me about a recent interaction. The issue was legitimate. The choice of time and place was, shall we say, unhelpful.

Choose a setting in which the people most likely to be impacted will be best able to hear the message. This does not mean that it's your job to make things easy on people, help them avoid discomfort, or even control the fallout. Just make sure the setting enhances, and doesn't overwhelm, the message.

If all these conditions are satisfied, you can likely crack open that big issue with relative confidence. It might not be easy. It might not be fun. But it just might be time to drop the big one.

HOW TO WRITE A SCATHING EMAIL

There are a few essential skills that every leader must learn on the job. These are the things that no one will teach you in school. One of the most essential is how to write a truly scathing email. This section covers all the necessary ingredients and competencies needed to compose a devastating digital missile.

Think of it like one of the Sith arts of leadership. No, you can't learn it from a Jedi. Here's how to do it:

First, be self-righteous. This is the foundational ingredient. In fact, I need to be so sure that I am right about my grievance, ideas, or position that conversation is not required. Absolute certainty requires no further information. Invitation to discussion would only carry the odor of compromise and the stink of doubt. No compromise. No retreat.

Second, be convinced that the above self-righteousness is actually good for the recipient. My radioactive email will be like a purging fire. Sure, it's harsh medicine. However, in the end my colleague will see that the email's lack of charity and sensitivity was actually a kind of mercy. Whether they knew it or not, this was something they needed to hear . . . from me . . . right now . . . at 5 a.m. This will show them just how important this topic is to me.

Third, include a long and exacting list of demands and/or solutions. These can be framed as "suggestions" if I'm in a particularly touchy-feely setting or I'm dealing with a genuinely kind and sensitive person. However, I've found that with enough of the self-righteousness baked into the text, they are sure to get the point anyway. Do not be brief. This is the opportunity to say everything that you've been holding on to and haven't shared over the last week . . . or year. Add multiple attachments if needed for extra evidence and clarity. An email like this is the perfect opportunity to clear the air, open those interpersonal windows, and let the sun shine in. Sure, the heat of that sun might be like picnicking on Mercury at noon, but it's all good. I'm doing this because I care.

Fourth, be convinced that this email will solve everything. Everything amiss in this relationship could possibly be put right with this one definitive act of communication. Because my email will be so blunt, thorough, and entirely lacking in nuance and compassion, the recipient is sure to fully understand the issues and needed remedies. They might even be grateful that I have saved us both from wasting our time with potentially lengthy interpersonal learning that comes with an actual conversation.

If you haven't picked up on my sarcasm yet, my lawyer told me that I must say explicitly:

Everything I have said thus far is exactly what you should not do when you have a serious problem to discuss with a colleague, or friend, or . . . anyone.

As I cover in the Fight Tip, Never Use Email, do not use text, social media, or other text-based messaging when delivering difficult messages or sharing strong emotion; the medium can make all the difference. In the previous section, *When to Drop the Big One*, I recommended four specific criteria to soberly consider before doing anything that will send massive shockwaves through a relationship or an organization.

And yet, there I was one day . . . Keyboard on lap, email composed, and about to hit send. Luckily, my wife happened to ask me what I was doing. With a wild gleam in my eye, I described the digital fury of truth I was about to unleash.

To which my wife said, "Isn't this everything you mentor people not to do?" It's dangerous to give people advice for a living. Someone might actually expect you to follow it.

There will be times when all of us are tempted by self-righteousness, arrogance, impatience, or generally thinking we have all the answers. No one is immune—including yours truly.

If you even suspect that you might be falling prey to any of the above traps, fallacies, and temptations, learn to pause and get a second opinion.

Find someone who knows you and has proven their ability to tell you that you are about to do the wrong thing.

This could be a friend or colleague, someone you supervise or a supervisor. Whoever it is, they need to be able to say, "No. Don't do that, dummy."

I have a small group of such advisors. Their titles and positions have nothing in common. The one thing they all share is that they care about me, know me, and will give it to me straight—every time. Don't ask for advice from an enabler or someone likely to tell you how right and brilliant you are as you boldly run off a cliff.

As providence would have it, one of my trusted advisors caught me that day and recommended that I re-read some of my own work. Touché. Well played. Mea culpa.

Email deleted. Face-to-face meeting scheduled. We are all still learning and practicing.

TOXIC WORKPLACE BEHAVIOR PROFILE

THE BLACK SWAN

Code Name: The Black Swan
Motto: Repent, for the end is near.
Favorite Song: "It's the End of the World as We Know It" by REM
Favorite Movie: *2012*
Behavior: Sooner or later in your career, a colleague will do something so outrageous, hurtful, strange, criminal, or over-the-top that it will make you question everything you think you know about people and relationships. Eventually, you'll meet a Black Swan.

The Black Swan is unlike all the previous toxic workplace behavior profiles due to one simple fact. The precise manifestation of the Black Swan cannot be predicted. This person is, by their very nature, a complete outlier.

Typically, the term "black swan" is used to explain exceptionally rare and disruptive events that have an unusually high impact on our lives and sometimes the course of history. Financial risk analyst and statistician Nassim Taleb asserts that these events are usually distinguished by three simple characteristics:

1. The event is a surprise to those involved.
2. The event has a major impact.
3. After the first known occurrence of the event, it is rationalized by hindsight, as if it could have been predicted. (See Taleb's book *The Black Swan: The Impact of the Highly Improbable*.)

The stock market crash of 1929, the 2004 Indian Ocean earthquake and tsunami, the 2011 Japanese earthquake and Fukushima meltdown, and of course the COVID-19 pandemic were all black swans for most of us. These events were surprises and are still having a massive lasting impact on people, systems, and society.

In the immediate wake of each event and ongoing until this day, there have been those who claim to have seen it coming, or more accurately, that we could have seen it coming if we had only paid attention to x, y, or z factors.

Though there is often much that we can learn in analyzing these types of events, there is one big, hairy, uncomfortable fact that is common to black swans: Claims to predictability typically work only in retrospect.

Uncertainty involves risk. Risk involves danger. And we are hardwired to avoid and minimize danger. This is why these events are so unsettling. Black swan events remind us of the ever-present possibility of unexpected radical disruption, and of our own fragility in their presence. Black swans are the ultimate loss of control.

In retrospective analysis, we are capable of great leaps of magical thinking to convince ourselves that we could have seen "it" coming and thus can predict the next specific event. Pandemics, economic crashes, earthquakes, nuclear meltdowns, and tsunamis are terrifying prospects. Each of those events will impact the world for years to come. But statistically, we'll likely experience only a few of those in our lifetime. We are far more likely to experience a black swan when it comes in the form of a person.

I once helped a midsize international company process and recover from the impact of a senior leader who had been systematically defrauding the company for many years. The scope of the fraud, the meticulousness in how the leader covered her tracks, and the failure of organizational safeguards were all gravely concerning. But none of these things were the most important issue for those involved.

The most difficult aspect of what this leader did to the company and to her colleagues was that her behavior was the complete and utter opposite of her public persona and reputation. They just couldn't believe that this person did it and that it happened in their company.

This disconnect threatened to tear apart relationships in the organization. After all, if this most trusted colleague could do something so terrible, then anyone could. The difficult thing this team eventually had to face was that this was, on some level, actually true.

Yes, in retrospect there were aspects of this person's past behavior that were viewed in a more concerning light once all the facts were on the table. Yes, the company might have had insufficient controls in place to maximally deter and flag suspicious behavior. These environmental factors certainly contributed to the likelihood of the fraud, but none of those factors were predictive of how and through whom that fraud would manifest. While most people expressed utter shock at what transpired, there were a few who claimed (in retrospect) to have seen this coming—just as Nassim Taleb predicted.

However, the hard reality was that this person was so disproportionately and uniquely skilled in hiding her behavior and projecting an opposite image, no reasonable person could have been expected to see it coming. The organization had met a Black Swan.

Sooner or later, you'll meet one too. Perhaps you already have. The specifics of a Black Swan's behavior can vary greatly. The most destructive behavior in the workplace, as in other areas of life, most commonly involves sex, drugs, or money—and frequently a dastardly mix of all three.

I have also seen what Edgar Allan Poe referred to as the "imp of the perverse." Poe used this metaphor to describe how an otherwise normal and well-adjusted person can suddenly do something harmful and irrational simply and precisely because it is the wrong thing to do—and with little warning. It's rare, but it happens.

However, potential Black Swan behavior is, by its very nature, unpredictable. I've seen unknown or undiagnosed psychological issues, destructive dualistic lives and personas, or simply a burst of bizarre and unpredictable Poe-like behavior play out in ways that are extremely difficult to forecast.

Do Not: It's largely futile to attempt to accurately forecast the precise "who and how" of this type of behavior. It is also typically a very poor use of organizational resources and psychological energy. Unless you are in the CIA, NSA, NCIS, or otherwise in the professional deception detection or crises response business, you probably won't be very good at this anyway.

In processing the aftermath of the story above, the staff and leadership realized that the only way to truly prevent all future events like this would be to treat every single person in the company as a potential Black Swan. That is exactly what some organizations do after such events. This always destroys trust and, eventually, the culture of the organization. A workplace where no one is trusted is worse than an organization that works hard on trust and absorbs the occasional act of malfeasance.

There is also an opposite temptation to believe that Black Swans are so rare, such an aberration, that nothing like this could ever happen again. Such responses to Black Swans are doubly dangerous. In these scenarios, staff are often pressured to move on without adequately processing the event emotionally and relationally, while also failing to rectify environmental factors that they can actually control.

Leadership must be careful not to give absolute promises that something like this will never happen again. Given enough time, it will. Instead, see below.

Do: As the organization I worked with did, focus on the following:

Be utterly and completely transparent with staff to the fullest extent possible. Notice that I didn't say to be transparent "to the extent you are comfortable." Be so transparent that it hurts and pains you. Don't break confidentiality laws or reasonable personal privacy or violate separation agreements. However, share as much information as possible about what happened with internal stakeholders, and sometimes in a more limited way with key external clients and customers. Withholding or otherwise obfuscating information always makes things worse, breeds rumors, and exacerbates fears. Don't fool yourself into thinking that you can contain the information. If more than one person knows, assume everyone knows. Lead the aftermath by making sure that everyone has an accurate account of what happened. If you are prevented by law, agreement, or other discretionary considerations from sharing certain pieces of information, say so and why.

Allow staff to fully process what happened, how they were impacted personally, their feelings, and fears. In the aforementioned case, many people shared that they felt personally responsible. Though they did not bear direct responsibility, many felt shame. Senior leaders were ashamed that such a thing happened in their company. Staff who were close to the Black Swan were afraid that others would suspect them as well. Others were struggling with unrealistic expectations that they personally could have prevented all this from happening. And a lot of people were simply sitting with a big ball of anger, sadness, and disappointment that they didn't know how to handle. Making generous amounts of time available for these conversations to play out didn't fix everything or take away the pain.

However, it did allow people to reality test their thinking and share the emotional and psychological burden.

Admit that while you can't make absolute promises that something traumatic will never happen again, you can fully process and address some of the factors that contributed to it. The company above revamped its financial procedures and safeguards, changed aspects of the chain of command and supervision, and instituted a range of new norms and expectations regarding how to handle and communicate red flags in behavior and processes. All those improvements were worth implementing in their own right, even if the Black Swan had never appeared. In this way, the company became stronger in the wake of the trauma.

Be willing to revisit these conversations over time, while progressively moving forward. It can be a mistake to stay stuck in processing the same trauma over and over again. Regardless of what happened, everyone has a job to do and people that depend on them to do it. Don't let your team become paralyzed. However, people process difficult events in different ways and on diverse timelines. The person who seemed stoic and unperturbed at the first meeting might be crying in your office two weeks later. The unit that was cool and collected handling the crisis at the outset might start falling apart in two months. You must make it OK to not be OK, embrace the suck, and give people permission to talk about what happened as needed.

Black Swans happen. You cannot predict exactly when and where they will appear. However, using these habits, you can build a team culture that is resilient, realistic, and ready to handle whatever flies into your little pond.

PRINCIPLE 6:
GROW IN PUBLIC

It's hard to grow when others are watching. Even if we know that change is needed, there's something we need to get better at, and other people are depending on us, part of us always resists.

Personal change and development feel risky. When we admit that we need to change our behavior, habits, skills, or worldview, we expose ourselves. It's an admission that something about us is incomplete and unfinished. This shakes us out of the comfortable fiction that we are wholly competent, fully baked, complete.

All the great leaders I've known in my life rebelled against the comfortable fiction of "finished-ness." They were people forever in motion. Always growing. Centered, yet restless.

Once you:

- develop the ability to Move toward Fear,
- accept that There's No Nice Way to Poke Someone in the Eye,
- Embrace the Suck that comes with engagement,
- decide to Fake It until You Make It, and
- learn how to Be Radically Transparent,

then you're really ready to make serious changes in how you engage with those around you. However, everything of great value requires great effort and risk.

These principles will set your development in motion and create new relational situations and opportunities that demand growth—in others, yes, but mostly in you.

As I covered earlier, most conflict is creative and can actually be fun and healthy. And with the right mindset, you can even engage with the most toxic personalities and situations with willful cheerfulness if you have the best interests of others at heart.

Are you being bullied by someone? Is your supervisor a tyrant? Are your ideas and input steamrolled at meetings? Is a toxic personality making you dread showing up for work? Do you have a radically different vision about a team project?

If any of those scenarios ring true, then change will happen only when you are ready to act, risk, and, hardest of all, grow in public.

In *An Everyone Culture: Becoming a Deliberately Developmental Organization*, adult-learning and organizational-change experts Robert Kegan and Lisa Lahey explore the unique features of organizations proven to maximize employee potential and achieve exceptional creative results.

From hedge funds to tech start-ups to nonprofits, Kegan and Lahey discovered that "deliberately developmental organizations" (DDOs) have cultures that encourage radically honest self-reflection and responsibility taking—not only for one's work but also for one's relationships and personal growth.

DDOs accomplish this through intensively collaborative and horizontal employee engagement practices that encourage group learning, decision-making, risk-taking, and confrontation—regardless of title or position.

However, these organizations also utilize vertical lines of authority that, instead of micromanaging and interfering with the daily functions of units and teams, keep leaders focused on ensuring that lower levels of the organization are taking active responsibility for decision making and personal growth in pursuit of the organization's goals.

When leaders focus their time and energy on building a culture that reinforces these consistent relational principles, both people and bottom lines tend to grow exponentially.

A deliberately developmental culture is made only by cultivating deliberately developmental people. This requires leaders who are willing to share what it is about themselves that is under development—and to do so publicly.

This also requires humility—the same humility that others on your team will need if you expect them to be honest about the parts of themselves that are still under construction and in motion. Like Bob Dylan once said, "He not busy being born is busy dying."

Leaders willing to grow in public show team members that discussing one's rough developmental edges is an act of strength and confidence, not a sign of weakness or ineptitude.

This helps everyone to take off the mask of completeness and embrace the reality that every individual and team is a perpetual work in progress.

FIGHT TIP

BLOW UP THE CONVERSATION

Encourage "growing in public" by expanding participation in conversations that matter—especially those involving conflict between colleagues.

Typical managerial responses to workplace conflict tend to treat conflict like a disease.

Managers usually try to isolate those involved. The conversation is kept out of view and in a separate space, sealed off behind closed doors so it doesn't infect the rest of the organization.

To lead conflict, you must do the opposite. Blow up the conversation by expanding the scope of participation and making it more public.

Do this by asking yourself and those directly involved, "Who else needs to be a part of this conversation?" and "Who else is impacted by this?" Doing this consistently will encourage productive engagements, not make things worse.

When you expand the range of stakeholders involved in a conversation, especially a difficult one, you multiply the problem-solving power exponentially.

A well-selected group also reduces the likelihood of outrageous behavior through increased social pressure and support. Of course, don't pick the five biggest hot heads, throw them in a room, and hope for the best. That might be entertaining, but it won't be productive.

Instead, include a mix of skills, personalities, and perspectives. Just make sure each person has a stake in the discussion and a relationship with those at the center of the conflict.

Do that, and you'll demonstrate to your team that you can lead when they need you most.

GROW OR GO

Eventually each of us, or someone we supervise, will be faced with a professional crossroads: it's time to grow or time to go. This is the point at which we recognize, and hopefully accept, that the skills that got us here will not be sufficient to get us there.

While true of everyone in an organization, leaders in particular must avoid the temptation to seek permanent stasis and the illusion of perpetual competence. Instead, great leaders consistently seek the "broken places," gaps, and underdeveloped areas of their practice as leaders. Huge performance dividends are paid to leaders that engage these areas proactively, boldly, and strategically. That, in essence, is leading conflict. Here's an example.

Many years ago, I was helping to develop a new unit in my organization. The organization was growing rapidly, and we hired several new staff to meet the growing demand for our services.

One new staff member had a perfect resume. He was technically proficient, worked hard, and was exceptionally conscientious. He was willing to work extra hours when needed and readily communicated needs, updates, and suggestions for improvements to leadership. Sounds like a perfect hire, right? Not necessarily.

This organization's culture was very distinct. It was supportive and nurturing, but it also demanded intensive collaboration and interpersonal risk-taking. If it was an ice-cream flavor, it would be maple-bacon. It's a specific thing. It's not for everyone. For some, it's a very acquired taste.

In this organization, it wasn't enough to be personally brilliant or effective. Staff were asked to also commit to maintaining the unique culture, collectively developing norms for work and behavior and building their interpersonal competencies.

If you're the type of person who just wants to show up, put your head down, work hard, and be left alone, this probably wouldn't be the place for you. Such was the case with the new staff member mentioned above. He didn't like going to so many meetings. He thought the regularly scheduled team-building activities were a waste of valuable work time. He didn't like talking about or being around particularly strong expressions of emotion.

Leaders regularly called brainstorming meetings to gather improvement suggestions from staff. He found these sessions exhausting. He openly said that those in charge should just make these decisions on their own and stop interrupting the regular workflow for everyone else. "After all, isn't that what leaders are paid to do?" he would often challenge.

Additionally, this organization had no formal disciplinary processes for low-level conflict between employees. Instead, leadership typically facilitated face-to-face meetings to assist staff in repairing relationships and responsibility-taking when things went sideways. This new staff member also disagreed with this way of doing things. In his opinion, supervisors should just give the person a formal reprimand. "If they don't change, just fire them" was his common refrain.

These reactions were all things we'd heard before, or even said ourselves when we first joined the organization. Leaders were used to being patient with new staff. Since most new hires were used to "high-monitoring" organizations in their previous work experiences, suddenly entering a demanding high-trust culture could be jarring.

It often took a while, a few months to a year or more, for new staff to fully adjust to this way of doing things. It took time to trust that this wasn't just a bunch of psycho-babble smoke and mirrors—that it's all for real. This staff member had been with us more than a year. They had plenty of training, practice, opportunities to challenge and ask questions, and support from colleagues. Eventually, it became clear that it wasn't that he didn't understand or trust our culture. He just didn't like it.

During one critical conversation, the staff member said reflectively, "You know . . . I think I would just rather work in a place where I can show up, do my work, and not be bothered with too much interaction with other people if I don't feel like it."

"Fair enough," I said. "But you can't do that here."

Mind you, this staff member did great work when it was something he could do alone. He was honest and hard-working. We valued all these things. However, the "people part" of our culture was just as important as excelling at tasks, and it wasn't optional.

With some relief, this staff member asked if we would help him with a plan to leave. For the next several months we gave him ample flex time to attend interviews. He even happily trained his replacement, also giving them a fair and honest heads-up on what to expect from the culture.

There were no hard feelings and no drama. We wrote him some great references. We even asked if he'd participate in a "goodbye circle," which we offered to all staff when they chose to leave. We even usually offered the opportunity to do this when someone was being fired. Each colleague shared something that they valued and would miss about him. He thanked others who had supported him, including the leaders with whom he'd struggled at times and who had helped him find another job.

Culture is a powerful thing. It's also delicate. That's why occasionally it's time for a colleague to choose: grow or go.

FIGHT TIP

TALK TO THE EMPTY CHAIR

In the Toxic Workplace Behavior Profile: The Black Swan, I discussed how harmful and highly disruptive behavior can manifest unexpectedly in the workplace . . . and sometimes from the people we'd least expect.

I shared a story about how one company responded in the aftermath of their own Black Swan experience. Many people were simply sitting with a big ball of anger, sadness, and disappointment that they didn't know how to handle. How do you encourage a group to grow in public and learn from this kind of an experience?

One of the suggestions was to allow staff to fully process what happened, how they were impacted personally, their feelings, and fears.

Several staff wanted to confront the Black Swan directly and tell her how she had harmed the company and hurt them personally. The problem was that the Black Swan was gone. She had quickly separated from the company, was coping with her new legal situation, and had no interest in talking to anyone she had hurt.

Since a face-to-face interaction wasn't possible, we tried something a little different.

We made a circle of chairs and left one empty. Everyone then took turns talking to the empty chair as if they were talking to the Black Swan personally.

Participation was voluntary. It felt weird and awkward at first, but people began to say all the things they wished they could say to her directly. Many were very angry. Some were just sad and hurt.

A few said they were concerned for her as a person. After all, some of the people in the circle had thought the Black Swan was their friend.

Talking to the empty chair didn't fix everything, but a lot was said that otherwise would have been kept inside.

The biggest takeaway from the experience was that while the Black Swan had hurt everyone terribly, their company would recover and move on as a community.

Their Black Swan encounter was traumatic, but they were willing to face what happened and the personal impact. They supported one another instead of passing blame and tearing relationships apart.

In the end, they learned a lot about themselves as a group and developed some of the resilience they will need when the unexpected appears again.

HIGH-MONITORING VERSUS HIGH-TRUST WORKPLACES

I once worked as a counselor in an alternative school for delinquent and troubled teens. The building was full of young people who were on probation, expelled from their home school districts, or facing other serious disruptions at home. This program was (and still is) universally known as one of the most effective in the region for producing remarkable behavioral and life changes in the youth we served. The day-to-day environment was also remarkably different from nearly every other similar program at the time.

For instance, we were a "hands-off" program. We didn't restrain or otherwise manhandle our students. We didn't manage behavior through on-site medicating. There was no graffiti on our walls. You were unlikely to hear profanity. Fights and violence were extremely rare. There were no metal detectors or video cameras. We had no guards, and the doors were unlocked.

Here's the kicker: we had no code of student conduct. Instead, we had five simple prohibitory rules that everyone was asked to memorize and follow. These were the five big non-negotiables.

They were:

1. No violence or threats of violence to people or property
2. No leaving school property without permission
3. No sexual activity
4. No drug use or suspicion of use
5. No stealing

That's it. Mind you, we were also tough. If you couldn't abide by any of those clear rules, you couldn't stay. We gave students opportunities to make mistakes and learn from them, but you couldn't actively violate those rules and keep showing up.

We made it clear that when you walked through the door, you were personally making the decision to follow those expectations and hold your friends and classmates accountable to them as well. There was no middle ground.

Everything else regarding behavior we turned into a community conversation that we helped the students negotiate and discuss with one another on a regular basis. This school culture wasn't something we did to you. Instead, this community was something in which you had to be ready to personally invest as a student.

Other than the five non-negotiable things we asked people not to do, we focused all our energy on what everyone should do—all the areas in which everyone (staff too) was expected to "grow in public."

We spent a significant amount of time talking about "norms" for behavior and expectations for everyday responsibilities, such as classroom activities and cleaning up after lunch. On the staff side of the culture, we created a set of affirmative commitments we called "basic concepts." Then, we behaved as if we expected everyone to do the right thing (even when skeptical) and expressed surprise (even when not surprised) when they didn't. We used instances of bad behavior as an opportunity to publicly reinforce our highest aspirations for one another, rather than a rationale to expect less from those around us in the future.

Misbehavior was not cast as a violation of policy. Instead, it was harm done to your relationships, classmates, and community that you now had a responsibility to repair. In a culture like this, impersonal detentions and such serve no useful purpose. You had to face the real people you hurt, take responsibility for what you did, and find a way to rebuild trust. When done right, this is far "tougher" than simply being punished by authority figures.

Staff set strong boundaries and had a say, too, but this was ultimately the students' community. As we told them many times, they had the power to make that community whatever they wanted it to be. Each day these young people had to decide just how serious they were about making a change in their lives. If you weren't serious, this wasn't the place for you. We'd even help you find another place to be.

This way of doing things is not easy. It requires intensive daily effort from everyone in a community. However, this active co-creation of a real community is what unlocked the hidden potential of our students—as leaders and as human beings. Sure, we could have forced them into compliance with our expectations by monitoring their every move and applying sanctions when we discovered violations. That's what most programs for troubled youth did and still do.

Instead, we did the painstaking work of helping them form a community that they actually valued and that made them want to do the right thing in the first place, whether adults were watching or not. Workplaces must make a similar decision about their internal cultures. You can either have a high-trust culture or a high-monitoring culture. You can't have both.

Each way is a lot of work. There's no free lunch. However, each approach is based on fundamentally different and opposed assumptions about the nature of work, people, and their potential. Here are a few contrasts:

High-monitoring workplaces:

- Give poor performance and bad behavior most of the attention and, thus, influence over the culture.
- Encourage mass compliance.
- Value obedience over learning.
- Proliferate rules and procedures.
- Create vicious cycles of monitoring, sanctions, and regulation.
- Erode trust by suppressing public responsibility-taking, learning, and growth.

High-trust workplaces:

- Give exemplary performance and good behavior most of the attention and, thus, influence over the culture.
- Value initiative, including questioning the way things are done.
- Value learning over mere obedience.
- Minimize procedures and rules.
- Create virtuous cycles of self-discipline, peer correction, and personal freedom.
- Build trust by encouraging public responsibility-taking, learning, and growth.

I have a friend who is a brilliant guy. He attended excellent schools and has off-the-charts aptitudes in the field of IT. He's conscientious, creative, and trustworthy. Yet, his entire job description is this: all day/every day he monitors the online behavior and time-on-task of his colleagues within a large corporation. All of this is done from a keyboard at home using advanced software and performance metrics. The data he gathers is congealed into digestible reports and sent to other managers, who then punish or reward their staff accordingly.

In any culture, behavior will tend to congregate around the standards and benchmarks that are discussed the most. High-monitoring cultures focus on minimally acceptable standards. Accordingly, they promote mediocre and minimally acceptable performance. This behavior-management strategy is fundamentally the same as most programs for troubled youth. Because a few people can't be trusted, they treat everyone in the culture as unworthy of trust. Everyone then adjusts to those expectations.

Conversely, building a high-trust workplace culture demands that we treat others as trustworthy. Only then are most people likely to rise to meet that expectation. Sure, some won't rise to the occasion. But most of those people are likely to behave that way no matter where they are. Don't build a workplace culture around loosely committed and low-performing outliers.

By all accounts, my friend's company is financially successful. However, what is it like to work in a place like that? What type of people and leaders does it develop? How much personal growth does it encourage? How much potential creativity and innovation are lost by focusing brilliant professionals like my friend on the task of catching a small minority of his colleagues doing things wrong? Even more important, how much more success, both human and financial, would this company realize if they focused on helping the vast majority of their staff to maximize what they can do right? With a high-monitoring culture, they will never know.

Much rests on which path an organization chooses. The decision will determine who and how they hire. It will determine whether internal resources are invested in preventing loss or encouraging gain. Most of all, this decision will communicate whether you are offering people only a life-deadening job or a potentially life-changing community in which to grow in public.

FIGHT TIP

ROCK, PAPER, SCISSORS . . . ELVIS!

My six-year-old son and I created a game. It is, in fact, the best, most fun game in history (at least according to my son).

It's called "Rock, Paper, Scissors . . . ELVIS!"

The beauty of this game is the rules—or lack thereof. Basically, the rules are the same as regular "Rock, Paper, Scissors" but with one tremendous wrinkle.

You start by saying: "Rock, paper, scissors, Elvis . . . shoot!"

And then, in addition to the usual choices (rock, paper, or scissors), you can say anything else that comes into your head. You also have to act out whatever you say. You can use your whole body, not just hand gestures.

We all know that rock breaks scissors, paper covers rock, scissors cut paper—but does rock beat Elvis? Does paper cover octopus? Can scissors cut lightning? Does school bus beat wizard?

Usually, the answer is . . . I have no idea. You have to go with your gut, debate it, or think about it. You can't operate on autopilot.

When two unexpected and ridiculous pairings are made, my son and I have to make a quick judgment as to which one wins. This task necessarily requires unusual creative thinking. It breaks you out of the well-known rules of the game.

By injecting creativity, something rote and predictable becomes something energizing and unexpected.

In fact, the more ridiculous the pairings, the more fun the game becomes.

Most workplace conflicts are mundane and repetitive. Once again, someone dominates the meeting and doesn't let others talk. A coworker sends another nasty-gram via email but doesn't talk to anyone face-to-face. There's hurtful gossip going around. (I'm looking at you, Submarine.)

And each time, we respond in the same way and nothing changes. Or maybe, as usual, we fail to respond at all.

Do the unexpected this week. Help someone, maybe you, to grow in public. When someone throws scissors (hopefully not literally), throw pudding. When someone throws paper, throw manatee.

In other words, use a skill or response you've never used before. Do something new that will break the usual patterns of behavior for you and others.

If you need to confront someone who has repeatedly failed to respond to one-on-one conversations, make it a group conversation. If lecturing isn't getting results, which it rarely does, tell the team you want them to generate the solutions this time.

If you tend to take over during conflict, hang back and let other leaders emerge. If you are usually reserved, assert yourself this week.

Often, an unexpected break in the routine responses to conflict is all it takes to generate a new and interesting result. Harness the power of the unexpected.

When it comes to growing in public, be The King.

COMPETENCE BEATS CONFIDENCE

Marvin was the best street fighter I've ever seen. The crazy thing is, you would never pick him out of a crowd as the top slugger. In fact, time and again, I watched bullies target him for harassment or a beating. It never ended well for the bully.

Marvin was not very tall at about 5'8". His weight was average. He usually sported a small paunchy beer belly, but he wasn't heavy. He wasn't muscular either. To top it off, he usually wore bottle-thick corrective glasses.

If you were a human predator, this is precisely the guy you would single out as the weakest of the herd.

Marvin and I attended the same private military college. Our corps of cadets was organized into companies: Alpha, Bravo, Charlie, and so on. We belonged to Charlie Company. Every company had a mascot. There were the Alpha Alligators, the Delta Dogs, etc. Our mascot was the Grim Reaper, or as we called him, Charlie Reaper. We did our best to live up to our dark and fearsome avatar.

There were lots of tough people at our school. There were many big Irish Catholic brawlers from the streets of Boston, rednecks from the backwoods of Maine, and tough-as-nails French Canadian hockey players. There were combat-ready women who would give Chuck Norris nightmares. There were sports heroes and future special operators practicing fourteen ways to kill you with a spoon. Marvin, however, was the undisputed fisticuffs master.

In those days at this institution, your company was your family. Think of it like a fraternity, but with much more brutal hazing and populated by trained soldiers. Rivalry between companies was intense and often violent. It was kind of like Hogwarts with combat boots and lots of whiskey. Good times, if that's your thing.

People in our company sometimes teased Marvin, but he was our brother and my friend. And if there was one rule above all others, it was that you defended your brothers and sisters from any threat and at any cost.

Like the neighborhood I grew up in, you could tease your own brother, but justice would swiftly descend on anyone else who did so. Early in our not-so-scholarly careers, a bunch of us from Charlie Company were at a party. It was getting late, and like most parties back then, things sometimes took a turn for the ugly and violent at that point. We were preparing to leave.

A big guy in the crowd from another company starting mocking Marvin. It was easy to do and didn't take a lot of creativity. A drunken moron could, and frequently did, mock his looks and the way he talked.

Marvin tried to ignore the guy and brushed him off a few times. The beer-soaked idiot got more aggressive and started moving toward Marvin. Several of us stepped between them. Not yet having seen Marvin in action, we figured he was going to need defending on a regular basis, so we'd better start now. Marvin put a hand on one of our shoulders, took a few steps forward, and calmly said, "It's OK, guys." At just that moment, the other guy took a swing.

Marvin neatly ducked that punch. We then watched in shock as Marvin proceeded to utterly dismantle the dude. It wasn't even really a fight. It was more like a controlled demolition.

The other guy seemed to be in slow motion, while Marvin was a blur of street-boxing precision. In less than a minute, a guy twice his size was on the ground with one hand up, begging for mercy.

Marvin granted the mercy. He didn't gloat or posture. He wasn't even breathing hard. He just turned to us and said, "All right, let's get out of here." We stood frozen, mouths agape in astonishment, as he walked out the door like an action hero.

Word spread fast. Very few people picked fights with Marvin after that, and he never started one. Many times, when someone started to tease him, someone else would quickly intervene with a subtle warning not to push things too far.

Two years later, a tall, lanky, and well-muscled guy who looked exactly like former heavyweight champ Michael Spinks in his prime decided to knowingly test Marvin on the central parade ground. Even though the guy was kind of a jerk, I repeatedly warned him to walk away. He didn't listen. About a hundred cadets watched as Marvin took him to school in another flawless performance. The other guy showed some heart, getting up two or three times more than he should have. But eventually, Marvin again showed mercy and told the guy, "Stay down, man. We're done."

There are some people you just don't fight. Marvin was one of them.

What does all this have to do with leading conflict? Well, a few things.

1. **If you see a short guy with thick glasses at a bar or a hockey game, it might be Marvin.** Don't fight him.
2. **Confidence is cheap. Competence is earned.** It doesn't matter how confident you are; it's competence that matters most. I learned this from the great boxing coach and former heavyweight fighter Martin Snow, owner of the superb and utterly old-school Trinity Boxing Club in lower Manhattan. Lots of confident guys challenged

Marvin. They quickly found out how much actual competence they lacked. The reality was, it made complete sense that Marvin was a skilled fighter. He had been teased since he was little. Instead of running and hiding his whole life, he decided to work hard to learn how to defend himself. When other kids were out partying and dating, Marvin was sweating it out in the gym and learning how to fight. He was also an accomplished wrestler. Most guys just want to look tough, not be tough. They work out so they sport big biceps and pecs. Marvin purposely and patiently taught himself how to fight, not just look like he knew how to fight. In the workplace, many leaders simply like what comes with being in charge: the desk, office, title, and other trappings. However, you cannot fake actual skill when leading conflict. The development of expertise requires that you put in the time, deliberately train to compensate for your weaknesses, and seek quality instruction. But most of all, you must believe that competence in leading conflict is something you can learn.

3. **Have a strong moral code.** Use your skills for good, not evil. Marvin frequently walked away from a fight or "backed down" but always because he wanted to and not because he had to. There were indeed times when he chose to fight instead of running away. But I think he understood that, sometimes, a well-timed display of prowess tended to prevent many future conflicts. This worked only because Marvin never used his skills to puff himself up or humiliate others. Marvin was a truly good person who never took joy in hurting other people, even if it was occasionally necessary. He also defended others when needed. Lesser men would have abused a skill set like his. Skill in leading conflict will only be useful in the long run if you truly have the best interests of others at heart. Think about how you can lead conflict effectively, to help not only yourself but your team and especially those who irk you the most.

4. **You must practice regularly and in real-life situations.** Life presented Marvin with plenty of opportunities to practice his skill set, whether he wanted to or not. Out of necessity, he tested everything he learned in real-life situations. There was no pretending. If something didn't work in a real self-defense situation, he discarded it. When learning how to fight at work, reading about the neuroscience of conflict is fascinating. Attending trainings on mindfulness and conflict resolution can be a wonderful experience. But when a coworker barges into your office and starts screaming obscenities in your face, will

you know what to do? If you know what to do, will you actually be able to do it? Identify what really works for you in your particular setting. Take what you learned from that book you read, that retreat you attended, or what you've learned here, and use it. Practice. Discard what doesn't work. Practice some more. Repeat.

Though his fights were memorable as technical spectacles, Marvin got in far fewer scrapes than many others over those four years. He had the calmness of one who knows he is truly competent. He also had the satisfaction of knowing how hard he worked to acquire those skills. He'd never had his hand raised in a boxing ring, but he was a true champ nonetheless.

Similarly, you are not likely to receive an official commendation or public recognition for your ability to handle tough interpersonal situations. Few organizations supervise and train these skills or reward such hard-earned competency at review time. However, when you put in the time to develop battle-tested expertise in leading conflict, you will find the inner peace that comes from accepting that you cannot control the world but you can be ready for it. You'll also notice innumerable downstream results, such as less persistent toxic behavior, deeper trust and respect, greater resilience, and the enhanced creativity that inevitably results from teams that aren't afraid of a little dynamic friction.

Learning is hard. Learning in public is even harder, but it's the only way to grow. There's no shortcut to competence.

TOXIC WORKPLACE BEHAVIOR PROFILE

THE PURITAN

Code Name: The Puritan
Motto: Let's just agree to disagree . . . so long as you agree with me.
Favorite Song: "The Sweetest Perfection" by Depeche Mode
Favorite Movie: *The Crucible*
Behavior: All communities, workplaces included, carry within them a dark potential to become so fundamentalist in their thinking and beliefs that any perceived digression is viewed as an existential threat. This type of toxic drift within the culture of an organization is usually driven by the behavior of one or more die-hard "Puritans."

The word "Puritan" originated as a pejorative term for sixteenth- and seventeenth-century English Protestant religious reformers who sought to "perfect" earlier reforms of the Anglican church. Many were undoubtedly people of strong faith with the best of intentions. These early Puritans were known for their piety, austerity with regard to behavior and displays of wealth, and disciplined adherence to their code of faith.

While none of those things are inherently toxic, elements of their movement saw a drift toward inflexible dogma, rigid social codes, and intense self-policing of their own congregations. Driving much of this was a commonly held belief that their small sect was a vanguard that would lead humanity to a coming golden age on Earth that would herald the end-times. In short, they sought to "purify" themselves, others, and institutions in anticipation of a coming quasi-utopia.

Though founded as a reform of the existing order, the Puritans were ironically very intolerant of other forms of belief and worship and thus at odds with most of their fellow Brits. Eventually, to the relief of themselves and presumably their neighbors, large numbers of Puritans fled to the Americas and founded the colony of Massachusetts and other settlements. In their new colonies, they couldn't even get along with the Quakers. I mean, come on . . . fighting with Quakers?!

History lesson over. Let's get back to the present.

What lessons can we learn about ourselves and workplace conflict from this little chapter of history? One lesson is that, while it's easy to

LEADING CONFLICT:HOW TO FIGHT AT WORK

beat up on some long-dead English colonists, the psychological dynamics that drove the troublesome Puritans lurk within all of us.

Whether religious, ideological, or procedural, we all have the potential to develop beliefs and opinions that we hold so passionately we begin to see dissent in others as an existential threat to our being, rather than an opportunity to engage and learn.

This dynamic is magnified when there is a co-occurring focus on achieving some form of organizational or communal perfection. In everyday organizational life, this might manifest as a commitment to a mission that is so intense that respect for the dignity and freedom of individuals is thrown under the bus on the road to the organizational promised land.

The more aspirational the mission of an organization, the more that organization is susceptible to this temptation. After all, if your organization is seeking to shape a better future for the world, right a dire injustice, or manifest a life-changing technology or innovation, what's a few human broken eggs on the way to your omelet of paradise? In one form or another, this is the typical argument of the organizational Puritan.

The Puritan is driven by false ethical logic powered by the belief that they serve a cause or ideology greater than themselves. The pursuit of this lofty cause is used to justify treatment of others that would be considered unethical in any other circumstance. Dreams of glorious ends are used to justify the use of horrible means in the present.

We can all fall prey to this behavior. Here are some other sure signs that we or others might be transforming into a Puritan:

Humorlessness. We begin to take ourselves and our ideas so seriously that we cannot laugh at ourselves or tolerate others poking fun at our beliefs. In my experience, this is symptom number one to watch out for, and a sure sign that someone is on the road to Puritan-ville.

Immunity to change. We begin to believe that we possess some kind of special truth or insight. The more we fall in love with our personal truth or ideas, the less we consider those things outside our own realm of knowledge. In essence, the Puritan becomes less willing to contemplate the possibility that they might be wrong or that their understanding is incomplete. At best, we stop seeking and evaluating opposing ideas. At worst, we actively silence and repress opposing viewpoints.

Immunity to correction. Critics are now seen as enemies, not just people with whom we disagree. When others have the temerity to challenge our increasingly humorless rigidity and unwillingness to consider alternative viewpoints, we lash out instead of listening.

Obsessive concern about the behaviors and thoughts of others. As the perceived threat posed by real or imagined dissent becomes magnified, policing others around us becomes a bit of an obsession. If the Puritan is moderately successful at repressing dissenting behavior, they often take a turn down the dark alley of imagining that they can police the thoughts of others. This manifests as an overconcern for any sign, however small or obscure, that others might not agree or otherwise think differently. This leads to . . .

Black-and-white thinking. You are either with me or against me. You either support the initiative or you are undermining it. Believe what I believe, or you no longer belong here.

Space for nuance and alternative ideas is lost. Organizations that fall prey to this suffer in the long term, as dissenters either go "underground," keeping potentially mission-critical insights to themselves, or they simply leave.

People stop saying what they really think. Instead, they say what they are supposed to think. This encourages groupthink and destroys creativity.

When this happens on a team or in an organization, you are left with an internal culture that might provide an intense sense of belonging for those who remain. However, this belonging is bought at the price of squashing the voice and agency of others.

An organization whose culture has become immune to challenge and correction from within will inevitably become unable to adapt to change in the outside world. The institution becomes inward-focused, rigid, and less relevant to those outside the bubble.

Do Not: The Puritan likely draws intense levels of meaning and purpose from their beliefs. You should not expect them to abandon their positions cold turkey and whole cloth. All-or-nothing, zero-sum, head-to-head, aggressive confrontation with the Puritan might feel good on some level, especially if you've been subject to their rigid rule.

However, this approach is likely to only confirm the Puritan's view of themselves as a bearer of truth in world full of enemies and unbelievers. Instead . . .

Do: Recognize and affirm what is true in the Puritan's belief system. When someone is desperately passionate about something, there is usually more than one kernel of truth in what they have to offer.

The error of Puritan thinking is not so much about believing outright falsehoods. Instead, the Puritan takes one or two truths and then myopically tries to view and interpret the whole world through that one lens.

Give the Puritan regular opportunities to be exposed to alternative viewpoints. Show them that they can hear someone else out without the world ending or without being forced to give up on their own ideas. In short, help them to be passionate while also being open to new information.

One concrete way to do this is to consider establishing shared ground rules for interaction and behavior within your team and organization. As I covered previously, one organization that I worked for called those ground rules "basic concepts." Others simply call these "norms." Regardless of what you call them, develop shared norms and behavior commitments that allow people to have strong personal opinions, while encouraging team members to respect the intellectual freedom and rights of others. The more different people are, the more those collective commitments matter.

How do I know so much about Puritans, you might ask? Sadly, I was one as a young man. It was sobering when I realized that I was the person that people were avoiding talking to during the proverbial holiday dinner. As my wise father told me on one such occasion, "John, if you expect everyone to agree with you all the time, you are going to wind up a very lonely person." Ouch.

When I realized that I was the Puritan in the room, I had two choices. The first option was to try to surround myself only with people who thought and behaved exactly like I did. Problem is, when you have a room full of Puritans, they typically turn on one another as they continue to find smaller and smaller things to disagree about. This is why radical political groups tend to splinter into ever-smaller, ever "purer" factions—until they realize that their rigid purity has made them toxic, unrelatable, and eventually irrelevant.

Puritanical habits of thinking tend toward perpetual deconstruction, not creation. You cannot build a healthy and sustainable community around a demand for ideological conformity. Intellectual monocultures are just as unstable as ecological ones.

The second option for me was to accept that the world is a lot more complex than I would like it to be—and then appreciate that as a good thing. In an organization, that complexity can often be uncomfortable, even disconcerting and disorienting. However, allowing for that complexity is precisely what is needed to learn and grow.

ROUND THREE
WINNING THE FIGHT BEFORE IT STARTS

OVERVIEW

The first three principles (**Round One**) of *Leading Conflict* help you overcome the natural tendency to flee from uncertainty and disruption:

- Fear of failure (Move toward Fear: Principle 1)
- Aversion to uncertainty (There's No Nice Way to Poke Someone in the Eye: Principle 2)
- Avoidance of suffering (Embrace the Suck: Principle 3)

The next three principles (**Round Two**) assume you are moving past the initial resistance to engagement and are ready to start taking more personal risks and looking in the mirror. This round asks leaders to move beyond simply engaging with the behavior of others and to focus on our own need to change.

- Feelings of "impostership" (Fake It until You Make It: Principle 4)
- Fear of exposure (Be Radically Transparent: Principle 5)
- Learning new skills while everyone is watching (Grow in Public: Principle 6)

The final three principles (Round Three) cover the core skills needed to be forward-thinking and strategic—to do all the above purposefully, in the best interests of others, and in support of an explicit vision for yourself and your organization. These principles require that you actively role-model what you are asking others to do. For instance:

- The necessity of *strategic* humility (Show Off with Humility: Principle 7)
- Embracing change and "disruption" (Seek Problems, Not Solutions: Principle 8)
- Winning the "fight" *before* it starts (Lead from the Future: Principle 9)

PRINCIPLE 7:
SHOW
OFF WITH
HUMILITY

Effective leadership is always part theater. This doesn't imply fakery or playing make-believe. It means that leadership is more than being competent, knowing what to do, and being willing to take risks. You also need to take action in a way that is purposely intended to teach others how to do what you know how to do, to transfer your skills and expertise to those around you through your personal example and modeling.

When I was a young counselor for troubled youth in a day-treatment alternative school, I prided myself on being direct and blunt. On the positive side, I had high expectations for the young people we served. Students trusted that I would tell them the truth. I didn't put up with lies or BS. If I thought you were using drugs again, I'd say so. If you acted outrageously, I'd be one of the first to intervene. I was never burdened with the desire that all the kids should like me. I wasn't there to be their friend. I was there to help them stay clean, get off probation, and learn a new way of life that wouldn't end in perpetual addiction, jail, or death.

In that setting, most adults walked through the door with a big heart on their sleeve. They didn't work for this program for the money or summers off. They were there because they wanted to help the kids who needed it most. When training new staff, we usually had to help people learn how to combine that care with a willingness to confront, set strong limits, and make people uncomfortable.

I had the opposite challenge.

One day, we had a particularly intense group session. We had been discussing behavior norms and dealing with the impact of some negative leaders in the student community, a few of whom I relentlessly called out during the group. When those handful of young people escalated the confrontation, I escalated right back. Eventually, those few students backed down, the group established some new standards for behavior, and we moved on.

After the group, an experienced counselor pulled me aside. He asked me how I thought the activity went that day. I said that it seemed like a successful group. After all, we "shut down" a few of the students who had been derailing things recently. However, I also sensed that the activity had gone sideways in some way; I just wasn't sure what was amiss.

Then he asked me an unexpected question: "Why do you do this work?"

A bit surprised, I responded, "What do you mean? I do this work because I care about these kids."

He nodded and then added, "Yeah. I believe you. I know you care about our students. I just don't think they know it."

I was floored. Part of me wanted to argue and defend myself, but I knew there was truth in what he said. This conversation was a turning point for me—in my growth as a counselor but also, frankly, as a person. We had a good long talk. This is what I learned that day:

- I was good at modeling how to be strong, but I was not comfortable modeling how to be vulnerable. I knew how to be right, but I didn't know how to be unsure. I consistently pushed people to improve, but I failed to communicate that I cared.
- I was good at keeping everyone in line but not very effective at teaching them how to change.
- Real learning, especially where personal behavior is concerned, requires vulnerability, willingness to let go of old certainties, and an admission that you need the care and support of others. I wasn't modeling any of that for our students. I was just the hard ass who'd bite your face off if you acted up. I realized that I wasn't as good at my job as I thought I was and that I still had a lot to learn.

The problem I faced at this point was that vulnerability, comfort with ambiguity, and all things touchy-feely did not come naturally to me. It wasn't who I was. The hard lesson I learned that day was that leadership isn't only about being "who you are." It's also about being who those you have chosen to serve need you to be.

Personally, I really didn't want to make any of those changes. Why would I? I was comfortable with who I was. The problem was, my current behavior wasn't helping our students. If I really cared about them, I needed to change. This forced me to be radically, if begrudgingly, humble. I honestly did not know how to get from here to there. I needed help.

My experienced coworker helped me realize that this was precisely the position our students were in. They had longstanding patterns of behavior that they didn't necessarily want to change, but they knew that they had to do something different if they wanted to move forward in life. He suggested that I be a lot more open about what is difficult for me in this setting and share my own plan for change with the students.

He assured me that this did not mean that I should be falsely humble or obsessively communicate my self-doubts. Instead, I should demonstrate that real courage and strength was a willingness to admit my weaknesses and commit to change. That was exactly the example these students needed to see in action.

"So," he challenged me, "do you want to be seen as competent? Do you want to be seen as strong while also communicating that you care?" If so, then I had to work on being the best at:

- Admitting my faults
- Talking openly about what I'm working on in my relationships and behavior
- Taking risks and sharing stories that are personal and humanize me
- Using my failures and self-correction as public learning lessons
- Fearlessly taking responsibility for my actions and decisions
- Making amends publicly when I act like a jerk (plenty of opportunities for this!)

None of this, he assured me, was an invitation to use my job as personal therapy. I should share only those things about myself and my own improvement that might strategically help our students in their own dilemmas and struggles. This demonstration of humility and transparency should be primarily for them and not me. However, that didn't mean I couldn't benefit as well. I certainly did.

This early experience in leadership taught me the valuable lesson that we cannot share what we do not have; we cannot teach what we do not practice. If these students needed to face their weaknesses, I needed to know how to do that too. If they needed to learn how to ask for help, I had to demonstrate how it was done. And most importantly, if change and learning required humility, I had to humble myself first.

As my career transitioned into leading adults, these lessons in humility—purposeful and sometimes strategic humility—were invaluable. It's a commitment to humility that separates the great bosses from the Boss-zillas.

FIGHT TIP

CHOOSE THE HIGHER STANDARD

In this section, we discuss the need to care for your online impression as carefully and strategically as you care for your in-person impression.

The digital and in-person worlds are no longer separate places. As a leader you cannot afford to pretend that you can set lower standards in one without impacting the other.

As you consider upgrading your own online image and social media strategy, consider this simple question:

How do you want to be seen by the people you respect the most?

When discussing this topic with my children, I ask them to think about their grandparents. As a leader, think about your mentors, valued customers, and those in your field who look up to you.

Does every aspect of your online persona and behavior reflect the best of who you are, as well as whom you want to become?

This is hard. It requires humility and discipline. You'll need to ask yourself who it is you really want to be, and just how dedicated you are to that vision.

Choose the higher standard. Be one person.

Every day, online and off, work to be the best version of yourself. Because that is who you really are and were meant to be.

BOSS-ZILLA: HOW TO NOT SUCK AS A LEADER

I love monster movies. The bigger and meaner the monster, the better the movie.

Alien. Predator. Kong. The Stay Puft Marshmallow Man. However, when it comes to on-screen destruction, the undisputed heavyweight champ and model for all monsters that followed is undoubtedly Godzilla.

Behind the cheesy effects and ridiculous rubber monster suits of the 1950s and '60s movies, there was a deep commentary on the tenuous nature of life in the atomic age. Godzilla's origin story has varied a bit over the years, but it's usually a nuclear accident or improperly handled radioactive waste that turns an ordinary lizard into a savage beast.

With great power comes great responsibility. Use nuclear science wisely, and it powers a nation. Use these abilities poorly, and they just might destroy us all. What does this have to do with leadership? Well, hang on to your popcorn.

Like the radioactive waters that turned a common lizard into a Tokyo-stomping terror, there are environmental factors in the workplace that can turn a would-be Mother Teresa into Maleficent or a nascent Winston Churchill into Genghis Khan. It doesn't matter if you run a hotdog stand or manage an investment firm, the dangers are the same. All leaders are prone to four common thinking errors. These errors arise from the stress, responsibility, and allure of power that comes with all positions of influence.

If you are in a position of leadership, allow me to be your Katsuhiko Ishibashi—the pre-Fukushima seismologist who warned the world about hardening reactors against the impact of earthquakes and tsunamis. I can only hope that, in this case, you will heed the warnings before it's too late. Don't become Boss-zilla.

As you plow your way up the org chart, if you find yourself turning green, growing scales, and developing a strange urge to annihilate a coastal city, you've likely been contaminated with one or more of these common and radioactive thinking errors:

1. You're taking yourself too seriously. Seriously, you're not that important. None of us are. Sure, no one wants to work for a slacker. However, people don't want to work for Napoleon either.

This is an area of leadership that takes practice and maybe even a little Zen-like perspective and insight. What's the sound of one hand clapping? I have no idea. I do know that well-balanced leaders take their work seriously and themselves lightly.

Be sure to spend quality time with people who do not work for you and don't care what you do for a living. Two-plus decades into my career, my two older brothers still ask me, "What is it exactly that you do?" I give the same answer every time. The fact of the matter is, they don't remember because they really don't care. They just want to spend time with their little brother. That's actually a good thing. Whoever those people are in your life, spend more time with them.

2. You're overestimating your impact. Competent and quality leadership is essential to any well-functioning organization. Try not to wreck the place, but also trust that your organization is likely a lot more resilient than you might think. Leaders come and go. Some are great, most are pretty good, and a few rare ones really suck. Try not to suck. Either way, life goes on and most organizations survive.

Even when you're not at your best, most organizations have other people ready and willing to fill the gaps, plug the holes, and keep things afloat. That's why you have a team and not just yourself. Trust your team and learn to lean on them when you know it's time to take a break and regain some perspective.

3. You're working out your personal issues at work. We all have issues. Many of these issues will play out at work on some level. That's only natural. However, you can't fix your trust issues with your spouse by over-monitoring your employees. If your parents didn't give you the support and attention you truly deserved as a child, that's painful. But it's not your staff's job to fill that hole. If you want unconditional love on demand, I recommend getting a German shepherd. I love mine and she is always happy to see me.

In other words, try not to use your organization as your own personal therapy-theater: replaying dramas from your personal life over and over again while hoping for a different result. Remember, a big part of the elusive work/life balance is the line dividing those two worlds. Take full responsibility for each and don't overmix the two.

4. You're substituting control for vision. I know . . . Everything would be great if people would just follow all your instructions and advice. Most leaders love solving problems. It's one of our defining characteristics. But if you're not careful, you might start thinking that every problem is yours to solve. Or worse, you might start believing that your solutions are the only right solutions.

Leaders who insist on controlling and micromanaging the small details of people's day-to-day work can debilitate an organization by short-circuiting learning and development. Just like you, your staff need the freedom to make mistakes. They also need the freedom to try out their own ideas. If you're lucky like me, your staff will prove themselves to be smarter than you are.

Instead of dispensing answers, help others to develop competencies. Instead of trying to control small details, set a clear and compelling vision and let your staff pursue it in their own unique ways. You just might learn a few things from them.

Be daring. Be bold. Be confident. But also heed these warnings. Don't become a radioactive beast. Tokyo is a really great city. Let's keep it intact.

WHAT DOES YOUR DIGITAL PERSONA SAY ABOUT YOU?

At a recent leadership and digital technology event, I participated in an interesting experiment.

The room was full of seasoned C-suite professionals and up-and-coming business leaders. We covered a diverse range of industries: pharma, biotech, higher education, IT, military/private security, supply chain management.

The facilitator asked us to make a list of keywords that described how we wished to be seen by others in our respective fields. The activity focused on the public identity and values we wished to portray to people meeting us for the first time, as well as those with whom we work every day.

For a few minutes, each of us worked alone to refine our personal list of descriptors to no more than ten items. Next, the facilitator asked us to pick a partner we did not know and tell our partner only our name, organization, and title. He asked us to keep our keyword list private for the moment.

We were asked to take out our laptops and spend the next twenty minutes performing a web and social media search on our partners. The facilitator suggested that we go beyond our partner's corporate "about us" page. Check their Facebook account and photos. How's their LinkedIn page? Read their tweet history. Have a peek at Instagram. Search their name and undergraduate college together as an image search. And so on . . .

He then asked us to make a second keyword list that described our impressions of our partner based on what we found online.

Finally, we compared how we each wished to be seen by others with what our online profiles and behavior portrayed to our partners.

Across the board, the activity produced some dramatic and diverse contrasts between the image people wished to portray and the one that their online profiles suggested.

At the mild end of the continuum, some described themselves as highly organized and motivated. Yet their LinkedIn page was only half completed and full of broken links. Others wished to be seen as entrepreneurial, yet there was no evidence of any innovative or risk-taking projects.

There were also some tougher lessons. Some described themselves as compassionate and emotionally intelligent collaborators. Yet their social media accounts were streams of anger, caps-lock invective, and opinionating that castigated entire swaths of people they might encounter in any workplace.

Others said they worked hard to be seen as serious, professional, and highly capable. Yet an online search easily produced photos of keg stands, blunt smoking, and other sundry party shots. By the look on some people's faces, I'm sure there were other more serious mismatches that were easily found with a casual web search.

Everyone was given time to process with their partners. It was a sobering experience.

Everyone in the room was highly competent and accomplished in their respective fields. In person, nearly everyone was interesting, kind, professional, and even inspirational. But the online personas frequently gave a much more mixed impression—sloppy or inconsistent at best, troubling at worst.

This activity led to a few key insights that were hard for many to accept but transformational for everyone's leadership development planning. Here's a distillation of the lessons learned that day:

Assume that everything you do and say online, and on every platform, is public. This includes all apps and social media. This includes comments threads, even if using your supposedly top-secret MemeLordX or ShitePoster23 moniker. Some of the more tech savvy folks in the room easily connected "private and personal" identities to professional ones.

Not only is all online behavior public, it is also part of a digital record that is difficult to edit or completely erase. For better or worse, the idea of the digital world as a private space is long gone.

Before you type and hit Enter, ask yourself, "Would I want my next big potential client, colleagues, or longtime customer to read or see this?"

Accordingly, don't say anything online that you wouldn't say in public, or to someone's face. Many people treat the digital world the same way they treat being in traffic on the freeway. People are much more likely to act outrageous when they are stuck in traffic with people they assume are strangers than when they are driving down their own street surrounded by neighbors. Read your average news comment thread, or even some of your good friends' social media feeds. 'Nuff said.

These platforms are designed to advantage emotion over reason, invective over argument, and sound bites over real discussion. Sound bite-driven emotional invective will indeed get you more shares, comments, and likes. It will also likely do more harm than good to your real-world relationships and professional image.

Every online platform is angling for a few more seconds of your attention. Simply put, extreme behavior and angst captures attention more easily than a thoughtful exchange. That's what generates clicks. And clicks are money. It's not personal. It's just business. But that doesn't mean it's good for you.

Understand that your online behavior *is* currently impacting your in-person relationships. This is an unavoidable certainty. Have you ever met an interesting person at a conference who pitched a great idea or potential collaboration to you? What's the next thing you did? You likely Googled them and did a little fishing. Others are doing this after they meet you too.

What they find online will impact how, and if, they decide to work with you. If there's something concerning there, most people will not address the issue with you directly. They might just quietly walk away.

Don't assume that just because no one is bringing up your online image, it's not a problem. The cost of poor online behavior can be tremendous and invisible. If you are not being your best self online, it will inevitably impact your professional life.

Be one person, online and off. Care for your online impression as carefully and strategically as you care for your in-person impression. This sounds reasonable, but don't underestimate how challenging it can be.

The illusion of anonymity, lack of immediate personal consequences for poor behavior, and availability of immediate emotional payoffs make many online platforms inherently addictive. Like any addiction, it might take you as long (or longer) to change that behavior as it took to develop those habits in the first place.

As we did at the event, begin by making a clear and accountable plan for change. This will entail some hard choices. Will your activity online be mainly professional or a mix of personal and professional? It used to be possible to do both separately. Today, not so much.

If you choose to do both, your old college friends, family, and crazy Uncle Willie will be mixed with the potential investor you just met and your new colleagues. There are multiple right answers, but the questions are hard nonetheless. Whatever you do, it should be on purpose.

Several people discussed permanently deleting their Facebook page or other social media accounts and starting fresh with a new focus and clear rules of engagement. Sometimes, the nuclear option is best.

Others realized that activities such as passionately discussing politics online (i.e., ranting) had developed into a major "hobby" that consumed incredible amounts of time and psychic bandwidth, with questionable payoff in the real world. Like an alcoholic thinking hard about not going to the bar every night, many of these leaders were literally distressed to consider how they would spend their nights if they chose to give up that behavior.

Your mileage may vary, but many of these incredibly busy people were shocked when they fully considered just how much of their time was spent chatting, posting, and trolling online—all for a negligible real-life ROI.

Time is a human's only truly nonrenewable resource. Make sure that you are using that social media platform strategically. Don't let it use you.

Been meaning to learn Spanish? Planned to start a blog or write a book? Need to be more present with your family? Eliminating compulsive and low-return online activity can yield massive amounts of new "free" time for the things that really matter.

Every successful business should have a clear and strategic online image, branding, and social media strategy. The increasing integration of the digital and in-person worlds means that every successful leader now needs one too.

BECOME WHO YOU WERE MEANT TO BE

In the next section, we'll read a story of a tough young man who had the courage of a real fighter.

At a crucial moment he chose to do the right thing, take responsibility, and sacrifice some of his own pride and comfort for the good of his community. He was a real leader.

Think about those areas of your work, relationships, and leadership that are calling you to make a sacrifice for the good of those you serve.

A wise mentor once told me that when you choose to be a leader, you trade one boss for many bosses.

What he meant was that leadership, the best kind, is that which puts all you have at the service of others— whether they appreciate it or not.

Like Carlos did, choose the more difficult path. It's the one that leads to the person you are meant to be.

FIGHT TIP

CULTIVATE THE GRATITUDE ATTITUDE

The great Jack Dempsey once said:

"A champion owes everybody something. He can never pay back for all the help he got . . ."

I pretty much live by that assertion. It's all the points of friction in my life and relationships that have helped me understand myself and figure out what's truest about people and the world.

Everything in this book represents a lesson, truth, or insight that I learned through and with others. We truly own nothing. All the best things in our lives come through grace and the generosity of others. Living this way keeps our ego in check and our eyes focused on those we aim to help.

LEADERSHIP LESSONS FROM A TEENAGE GANG MEMBER

I was walking up the stairwell to the main office like I did every morning. "How are you doing today, Carlos?" I asked with a smile.

"Doing great today, Mr. John," he said back with a sleepy grin. "Kinda tired though . . . I worked late last night," he said, stretching his arms above his head.

That's when I saw it—an oversized folding knife. Though fairly well concealed, the shiny metal clip inside his waistband was a dead give-away and caught my eye immediately. My first feeling wasn't fear; it was disappointment.

When working with tough kids, it's sometimes useful not to let them see what you notice at first. When there's a never-ending list of things that are not OK, don't seem right, or otherwise raise suspicion, you have to pick and choose your battles. This often gave me time to think and strategize. Carlos didn't notice that I'd seen the knife. He went off to class. I walked on and around a corner, then paused. Crap. What to do now?

At the time, this was one of the more dangerous high schools in New York City. Though relatively small, serving only a hundred or so students, the school population was made up entirely of young people attempting to transition from long-term detention, including juvie lockup on Rikers Island and other secure locations from around the various boroughs.

These weren't petty vandals and shoplifters. Most were affiliated with major gangs and/or the drug trade. Many had serious incidents of violence on their rap sheet; age was the only thing that had kept them from doing more serious time. A lot of them hadn't been to a "normal" school in many years. Many of them had basically grown up in the city's various detention facilities from a very young age.

The idea behind this particular school was to give these long-term detainees a transitional step back to their home schools. This school had a very high staff-to-student ratio, ample counseling, better credit recovery options, and a more consistent level of security than your typical large urban high school.

The students sent here would also, hypothetically, have a bit of insulation from their old relationships and conflicts back in their home neighborhoods. Not a bad idea on paper. In practice, things were a bit more complicated.

One thing the school planners hadn't fully considered was that when you brought students from diverse boroughs and neighborhoods together in one central location, you were throwing representatives and leaders from many rival gangs all together in the same place.

Some of these students' gangs were not on friendly terms with one another on the street. Others not in direct conflict saw this arrangement as an interesting new networking opportunity.

This was the school's second year of operation. After many months of chaos, the first year had ended in an evacuation after students set fires in multiple parts of the building. The entire staff quit. Literally.

The one exception was an experienced, street-smart, caring, and tough-as-nails ex-lawyer turned school administrator. She decided to have another go at this experiment and rebuild the school from the ground up. Most of the same students were returning. All staff had been replaced.

Gang life provides money, respect, and the other trappings of any criminal lifestyle. The most immediate benefits of being in a gang are a family to belong to, however destructive and violent it might be, and protection. But the tenuous ring of protection that a gang offers has limited boundaries, usually only a few blocks in practice.

Asking all these young people to come to an unfamiliar part of the city every day meant that they had to cross through multiple sections of "enemy" territory just to get to school.

This brings us back to Carlos.

I had been contracted by the school to help the staff and leadership build a safer and less chaotic school climate than the previous year. I was not a staff member, just a professional coach. The previous year wasn't disastrous only because the school was full of tough kids; lack of consistent vision and expectations from leadership as well as the consequent lack of cohesion among staff also contributed.

This year was different. Together, we started the year by having some hard conversations with administrators and staff, ensuring that everyone had the same expectations of students and each other. We also spent considerable time with students during the first weeks setting clear and firm bottom lines, while also letting them set goals and expectations with one another.

One clear commitment the students made to each other was to leave all gang activity at the door. The reality was, once students trusted each other enough to be honest, most of them were looking for a realistic off-ramp from gang life. Graduating from high school would be a good start. With that goal in sight for most, they set some clear rules for each other. Some of the most important norms they set were no gang colors, no drugs, and especially, no weapons in school.

They had jointly agreed to make the school a sort of "demilitarized zone" where they could set the usual stressors and dangers of street life aside. This wasn't something the staff could have imposed by their own will alone. Making these commitments real required a lot of painstaking and intensive work to help the students hash out these agreements directly with one another.

When Carlos brought the knife into school, he'd not only broken the law; he broke that agreement with his peers. The secondary risk was that, once others found out, they would feel the need to rearm as well.

For a few moments, I honestly considered saying nothing about the knife. Frankly, I'd come to depend on Carlos. He was a leader among the student body and was instrumental in helping to deescalate things early in the year. I had turned to him many times for help with tough situations among the students.

Part of me wanted to protect him. Another part of me just frankly didn't want to deal with it since things were going so well. If I'm being honest, I was also a little concerned for my own safety. Being known as the outsider who "ratted out" a respected student was not an appealing thought.

In the end, I chose to tell the leadership what I'd seen. They could make their own decisions about what to do next. That was their decision to make, not mine. They handled it well. However, it was Carlos who impressed me the most. Here's what he taught me about leadership that day.

He took full responsibility for his actions. The school leadership confronted Carlos directly, but also with care. As they suspected, Carlos was adamant that he didn't bring the knife to hurt anyone at school. He was genuinely contrite, and it was obviously important to him that the staff believe him.

He then talked about a situation that had developed outside school—an old beef from many years ago that had flared up again. He started carrying the knife because in order to get to school on time (which he did every day), he needed to travel through the neighborhood where he was most at risk of being hurt.

The school leadership was very sympathetic, but they were legally required to tell the school resource officer about the knife. Unfortunately, Carlos would be arrested and likely face a probation violation. Given his tough situation, it would have been understandable if he was angry and resentful. After all, in his own way he was trying to do the right thing by doing what he felt he had to do to get to school in one piece.

However, Carlos owned his mistake. He said that he had promised he wouldn't bring weapons to school and had broken his word. He said he should have reached out for help instead of trying to handle the situation alone. The staff assured him that they would've done everything in their power to help him if he had only asked.

Carlos took unqualified personal responsibility for his actions: a good lesson for all leaders from a sixteen-year-old.

He put the needs of the group above his own. Before Carlos left with the school police officer, he asked if he could meet with a few key students in the school. These students were leaders of other gangs and factions. Carlos said that he wanted to make sure that they knew the facts about what had happened and that he had not planned to hurt anyone at school. He wanted to help make sure students wouldn't start carrying weapons again.

To his credit (and my relief), he also said that he wanted to make sure the students didn't blame the staff for what happened; this was his mistake and his alone. The staff and students held a brief "circle" meeting. Carlos told them what happened, that he had a conflict on the street and was just trying to protect himself on the way to school.

Several other students spoke up and said how much they admired his courage in telling the truth and coming to talk to them face-to-face. Surprisingly, one of the leaders of a rival gang offered to talk to a few people outside school to make sure no one would bother him anymore. Next time, this student suggested, Carlos should trust him enough to tell him what's going on in the neighborhood so he could help (without violence).

He could have made himself into a victim for the students and inspired mistrust among one another and against staff. Instead, Carlos put the needs of the group above his own.

He did what he could to make things right. Carlos went the extra mile by not only taking personal responsibility and putting the needs of the group above his own but also offering to do whatever he could to make things right to both students and staff.

To the staff's credit, they said that the courage and maturity he'd shown in handling the incident was enough for them. Similarly, the students said they appreciated him telling them the whole story. They agreed that the situation could have easily escalated if the rumor mill was allowed to take over.

Someone suggested that, if/when Carlos returned to school, perhaps he could do something to make the student lounge and cafeteria area nicer. Carlos readily agreed and said that he'd think about it while he was gone.

He left school quietly that day with the police and returned to detention for a brief period. The judge involved with his case and his probation officer were shocked by how many staff intervened and sent letters of support on Carlos's behalf, attesting to his character and pleading for leniency.

A few weeks later, Carlos returned. The school held a short ceremony to welcome him back. Two weeks later, Carlos had finished installing an excellent music and sound system in the student lounge as a symbolic act of reparation to the community, as suggested by one of his classmates before he left.

I'm not sure what happened to Carlos after that year. I don't know what he is doing now. However, I've always remembered him when I'm faced with my own failings or I'm helping others face theirs.

He was a tough young man from an even tougher neighborhood. He had few of the supports I've enjoyed most of my life. And yet, at a crucial moment he showed the courage of a real fighter. He chose to do the right thing, take responsibility, and sacrifice some of his own pride and comfort for the good of his community. He was a real leader.

THE GURU

Code Name: The Guru
Motto: Be free by depending on me.
Favorite Song: Anything by Ravi Shankar
Favorite Movie: *The Master,* starring Philip Seymour Hoffman and Joaquin Phoenix
Behavior: All leaders must be teachers. However, on the road to becoming a great teacher, some are seduced down the fragrant dead-end alley of guru-hood.

We sometimes use the word "guru" in a way that is informal and innocuous. In everyday parlance, we might use the term to refer to someone we greatly respect, who has real expertise and a passion for helping others. That informal shorthand is not what I'm talking about here.

Instead, I'm talking about the murky line that exists just at the edge of being a great teacher. On one side of the line is an inspiring collection of experienced leaders who have devoted their lives to helping others to build expertise and apply it creatively in their own lives.

On the other side of the line, and just a few steps away, is a small collection of narcissists who inspire personal devotion and dependency instead of growth and development.

I've been involved in building education and coaching services for professionals for the better part of two decades. One time, early in building a new program, a colleague and I were in negotiations with the CEO of another company who was interested in collaborating with us on the project. This CEO was the founder of a well-known professional development platform. Over the course of several years, he had attracted a small group of committed students.

While we were getting to know one another, the discussions increasingly turned to our respective educational philosophies and modalities. In particular, it became apparent that this CEO was uncomfortable with my organization's openness to working with a diverse swath of professionals and leaders.

My organization offered very specific assistance in learning how to better form and manage relationships. However, we did very little picking and choosing of who we "allowed" to attend our professional development events.

In contrast, even though this CEO's organization taught very similar content, he insisted that instruction should be offered only to a select few. He believed that what he had to offer was so unique, so valuable and deep, that it should not be offered to "just anyone."

I responded that this stance might be more understandable if we were providing education around highly specialized topics that required concrete and specific background knowledge.

However, we were teaching relationship building, not string theory or nuclear physics. We certainly had a specific target population in mind, but as long as the professional had some humility and a sincere desire to learn, we saw no reason to turn that person away.

He was adamant. He wanted a special program for special people—even though he couldn't quite define just who these special people were. In fact, he concluded by asserting that even among the people that enter his program, "only about ten percent of them actually get it." By "it" he meant the depth of what he had to teach.

My colleague responded to the CEO, "Honestly, if only ten percent of your students understand what you teach, I don't think the problem is your students." Needless to say, that was our last meeting with this guru.

What can we learn from this little parable about the difference between teachers and gurus? Here are a few contrasts:

Teachers help students to believe in themselves. Gurus want people to believe in them. After an excellent learning experience with a great teacher, participants should be talking about themselves, the group experience, and what they learned. After a learning experience led by a guru, students tend to talk about how amazing the guru is . . . They will want to relive those feelings by being with the guru again and again, to get another fix.

Great teachers develop intimacy that moves toward equality. They want their students to eventually become equals and teachers themselves. Gurus have lopsided relationships marked by power imbalances that are forever tipped in the guru's favor.

Teachers simplify. Gurus mystify. I'm sure that the CEO with whom I was negotiating was telling the truth when they said that only ten percent of their students "actually get it." However, the guru's students didn't fail to understand because the guru was so deep. The students "failed" because the guru insisted on injecting artificial complexity into potentially simple ideas and concepts. He then used that complexity to keep his students "on the hook."

Teachers encourage freedom. Gurus breed dependence. Gurus keep the focus on themselves and create artificial complexity in order to promote and protect their artificial value. There's always an element of confusion and mystery when learning from a guru; there's always more around the corner, through the mist, or in the "next level" event. Register now!

Instead of examining the teaching method or teacher, students are encouraged to blame themselves if they do not yet understand. Thus, there's always another layer of teaching that guru needs to offer before you "fully" get it.

This breeds dependency at best and cultish devotion at worst.

Do Not: When facing a leader in the workplace who has positioned themselves as a guru, do not placate their delusions. Harsh as it might seem, my colleague's blunt statement—that the problem was the guru and not his students—was the right approach.

Do not allow a guru to be a master over their own institutional silo. Gurus crave a dedicated group of followers. They don't want students; they want acolytes. If given too much leeway, the bubble around the guru can thicken into an impenetrable fortress. Break down the walls.

Finally, do not expect the guru's followers to support you at first. Some people actually crave a relationship with a guru. It can be very attractive to believe that all one needs to do to be fulfilled, find purpose, or achieve success is to follow another "enlightened" human being in possession of some great knowledge, expertise, or secret. This allows the follower to trade the riskiness of personal development and responsibility-taking for the safety of personality worship.

Do: Make obvious and public examples that everyone in the organization must be open to challenge, examination, and questions—especially would-be gurus. Gurus and their followers tend to generate a toxic norm that the guru should not (or worse, cannot) be questioned.

Do the opposite. Challenge and question them publicly. In less serious cases, this alone can be enough to break the spell.

Put the guru in the position of student. Ask them to discuss their weaknesses and to be explicit about what they are learning and where they intend to grow. Insist they share these plans publicly with their team and those around them; that's something all leaders should be comfortable doing in a healthy and developmental organizational culture.

In the final analysis, always remember that any great teacher can be tempted to become a guru. The first piece of advice I give anyone who is setting out to become a mentor, teacher, or leader of others is this: Don't try to be famous. Try to be useful. Don't breed a herd of followers. Build a learning community instead. Be a leader, not a guru.

PRINCIPLE 8: SEEK PROBLEMS, NOT SOLUTIONS

Most leaders are trained to say that they seek new challenges, growth, and continuous improvement. It's fashionable to say that we see conflict as an opportunity. However, in practice most leaders avoid conflict and seek stasis.

Challenge, growth, and truly continuous development are inherently destabilizing. This is true when learning new technical, physical, or intellectual skills. It's triply true when learning new relational skills. Expertise in knowing when and how to upend the interpersonal apple cart has very little to do with head-knowledge. It has much more to do with practice, repetition, and discipline in doing what feels scary and unnatural.

You need to practice these habits and skills enough times to develop the instinct to do the opposite of what most people around you are likely to do. This is what's required in order to run toward an interpersonal fire as others are running away from it.

As we explored in principle 7, Show Off with Humility, we cannot share what we do not have and cannot teach what we do not practice. Actually, it is possible to teach what we do not practice, just not very well or credibly. Growth in relational expertise requires an admission that we don't know everything; we are all still a work in progress. If we are asking staff to "go there," we need to go there first and show them how it's done. That requires humility.

I'll hire a leader who actively practices humility over a genius-savant every single time. Without humility, expertise in leading conflict comes off as arrogance and manipulation. With humility, others will trust that even though you are asking them to do something scary, it's probably good for them.

Once you have a working knowledge and regular practice of the aforementioned principles, it's time to work on strategy.

Leading conflict means that you no longer live in fear of disruption. You stop being reactive, waiting for things to happen and hoping that nothing "goes wrong" today. Start engaging challenges proactively as a primary function of your leadership. This requires that leaders seek problems, not solutions.

As I said at the outset, regardless of what they say, most leaders seek stasis, harmony, and peace. Instead, seek the broken places, sharp edges, and underdeveloped areas of your organizational relationships and culture. Engage them. Don't solve them. Focus on what the team is learning from the challenge, not making the problem "go away" as fast as possible.

Aside from our own fears and insecurities, most workplace problems are really just creative challenges. Multiple people with good intentions are working hard to solve some technical, creative, or interpersonal challenge. That challenge might be difficult, but the interpersonal stakes are not that high. Often, the group just needs some confident leadership and a steady hand that isn't freaked out by the tension and disruption.

The tougher situations are toxic conflicts that center around particular personalities who are behaving badly and damaging workplace culture and relationships. These types of conflicts are far fewer in number, but they consume an inordinate amount of time and attention from leaders.

The primary mistake leaders make is this: when leaders are oriented toward seeking stasis, they will fail to adequately lead creative conflict and instead obsess over toxic conflict. When this is the norm, workplace culture suffers immeasurably. Those who behave the worst get all the attention. Those laboring to do the real creative work of culture-building are neglected.

Toxic conflict feels scary and urgent. In contrast, leading creative conflict feels optional because it carries less immediate threats. After all, creative conflict does tend to work itself out—even with lackluster leadership. Toxic conflict feels like it can boil over at any minute. This is where leaders must discipline themselves to do the unnatural thing and reverse this dynamic.

Spend the vast majority of your time engaging and leading creative conflict. This will proactively generate a culture that produces the new leaders you need and reduces future toxic conflicts through improved relationships and behavior norming. Conversely, be more sparing but far more direct in your response to toxic conflict. It is likely that 90 percent or more of your toxic conflicts are generated by just a handful of personalities—usually less than 10 percent of staff.

You know who they are and what they do. Leading conflict means you should have a plan for engaging each of those personalities on your (and the organization's) terms, not theirs. Don't wait for them to do the same thing again and again. Act. Don't react.

Be strong, bold, and determined in responding to toxic behavior. There should be only two options for these folks: an explicit plan for progressive behavior change or a plan to leave. This greatly simplifies the task for leaders and ensures that responding to toxic personalities does not dominate your time or organizational culture.

With a plan for engagement and clear goals for behavior change, these personalities should require no more than 10 percent of your time. If you are spending more time than that on toxic personalities, then these people are not the real problem—your reaction to them is.

FIGHT TIP

HUNT THE ELEPHANT

Don't worry. I'm not talking about a real elephant. I'm talking about a much more dangerous elephant: the one in the room.

There might not be an elephant in the room with you right now. You might feel relieved. You shouldn't.

This means that you don't know where the elephant is, because there's always an elephant in a room . . . somewhere in your organization. If you want to lead conflict, your job is to hunt it.

Go and find out what everyone knows but no one is talking about. Be the one to start that conversation next week.

In the next section, The Phantom Pooper, I share one of my most memorable consulting stories. We may never know the real motives behind the phantom's reign of intestinal terror. However, I'd bet dollars to doughnuts that some systematic elephant hunting would have made that phantom a lot less likely.

It's hard to talk about the relational things at work that cause us fear, anxiety, or just freak us out.

However, if you know how to move toward fear, poke someone in the eye, embrace the suck, and fake it until you make it, you know more than enough to get going.

Go hunt the elephant.

THE PHANTOM POOPER

I share this story with great trepidation, not only because of its scatological nature but because I fear it might leave you traumatized. However, some stories simply beg to be told lest we fail to learn from them.

No, the phantom pooper is not the world's worst supervillain. The phantom pooper is a real person, just like me or you, with a message for the world. That message is, when it comes to workplace conflict, you can bottle things up for only so long. Eventually, everything comes out. Let me explain.

I recently had an impromptu consultation with an experienced office manager. She oversees a large unit of staff within a vast and highly bureaucratic organization. This organization oversees a worldwide logistics and supply chain for advanced technology components. The complexity of this system is incredible. Its success requires intensive coordination between engineers, financial experts, and an international sales and requisitioning force. This manager's staff includes a wide array of very talented people.

Everything seemed to be going great this year. Then, someone pooped on a table. They also pooped in the lounge, in a hallway, and in a recently renovated staff room. I could go on, but I think you get the point.

I responded incredulously to her, "Surely there is something else at work here. Maybe you have a staff member with a medical issue of some kind? Someone who cannot control their bowels and is too embarrassed to tell anyone?" Oh, no . . .

She assured me that all the aforementioned pooping was quite deliberate. After learning the intimate details of each instance, it was clear that the phantom pooper was being very intentional in their choice of setting and strategic placement of each enigmatic deposit.

I have heard many harrowing stories in my many years mentoring leaders, but this one had a haunting quality all its own.

Leadership's only response to date was to invest in expanded video monitoring capabilities within their offices, in hopes of catching this rogue in the act. She asked me if I had any advice about what to do next.

I feared that, in my old age, this story would torment me like an aging detective's unsolved cold case. I needed to formulate a lesson, an action plan, or something worthwhile from this tale, not only for her but also for my future peace of mind. Here's what we discussed.

First, tempting though it may be, I suggested that we not focus on the whodunit aspect. She clearly had no idea who, from the hundreds of staff in the building, might do such a thing. If she did, they wouldn't be focusing on installing more video monitoring equipment in staff common areas. The reality is, she might never discover the true identity of the phantom pooper. Instead, we focused on the phantom's message as well as preventative actions that the manager could control and take immediately.

After some discussion, it was clear that this was really a manifestation of a much deeper organization-wide issue. In this large and sprawling organization, it was easy to become invisible and get lost in the expansiveness.

Though the organization was very successful as a whole, there was a tangible Borg-like quality to her descriptions of their culture. The mission and deliverables were very clear. However, I doubt that any one individual felt very important. When people feel invisible and unimportant, they will act out. Admittedly, pooping on the magazines in the staff lounge is extreme, but it does prove the point.

All humans have a basic desire to feel connected, to have a voice, and to feel like what they do matters and impacts the world around them. This requires more than just telling staff at meetings that you appreciate their hard work and asking them to give themselves a round of applause once a quarter.

Strong leaders make a regular habit of reflecting and sharing with each individual person they directly supervise how and why their contributions and voice are valued by the organization. It makes no difference whether that staff member is a janitor or a vice president. The personal needs and the conversation look exactly the same.

To prevent the next phantom, she and other unit managers needed to take a much more personal approach to supervision. If a colleague is so upset about something that they have literally started to crap on the company, it's safe to assume that these concerns (and potentially aberrant personalities) can be identified earlier.

I recommend that leaders use the following questions as a general format for this type of supervision:

- **How are you?** (meaning, the staff member personally)
- **How are we?** (meaning, your relationship with the staff member)
- **What would you like to talk about today?** Then share what you would like to talk about today to set the full agenda for the conversation.
- **Is there anything else I need to know (or that you/we need to talk about)?** Use this as a catch-all ending for the conversation.

Allow for silence and time to think in response to these questions. Gradually, but persistently, push staff to move beyond minimal and superficial responses. You want to actively surface problems and challenges, not avoid them.

Model the language and appropriate risk-taking by answering the questions yourself. Over time, expect staff to come to supervision ready to answer these questions with depth and clarity. Be prepared to really listen. Feel free to talk about your supply-chain performance measures, the quarterly budget, or whatever else is important that day. However, the aforementioned (or similar) questions should be asked during every supervision meeting and by every leader. This won't guarantee that a colleague will never go off the rails, but it does make it more likely you'll see the red flags and be able to intervene before they do.

Lastly, this organization had clear and explicit procedures for filing grievances, which people used prodigiously. An effective and fair grievance procedure has its advantages, but it offers very little in the moment to someone who is so upset, mad, or angry that they are ready to drop a deuce on your desk.

In addition to an understanding of the grievance procedure, make sure staff know what to do and whom to talk to when they or others are highly emotional. If you want to prevent bizarre behavior and unpredictable outbursts, there must be clear and readily available outlets for strong emotion. Don't miss the opportunity to lead directly in this area. Don't delegate this to the HR department. Whenever possible, lead these interactions directly within the context of your team and regular supervision. Then you can refer staff to other specialized supports as needed.

In addition to the supervision framework above, consider using versions of these same questions in larger staff meetings. As a way to surface tensions and other issues in the group, focus on the questions, How are you?, How are we?, and Is there anything happening in the team that we need to talk about?

Staff should know and trust that every team meeting, as well as personal supervision, will include some version of these questions. This will help exorcise would-be phantoms from your workplace. It will also ensure that when something freaky does go down, you'll have a pretty good idea about who is behind it.

FIGHT TIP

LAY IT DOWN; OFFER IT UP

A friend of mine frequently talks about his beloved grandmother. Though she's long since passed on, her lessons to her grandchildren still reverberate.

Like the lesson from my father that I share in the next section Horseshoes and Hand Grenades, the things that are really true in life tend to stick in the mind.

My friend's grandmother had a saying that always stuck with him when he was carrying a great burden, pain, anger, resentment, or even a secret.

Her advice was to "offer it up."

She was a very religious woman. Accordingly, her advice meant that when a burden feels too heavy, sometimes a leap of faith is required to unload it by trusting it serves a higher purpose.

When we carry knowledge about serious ethical or moral failings of ourselves or others, those burdens only get heavier over time, not lighter.

For leaders and organizations, a key obstacle to unloading these burdens is the desire to control everything that happens after disclosure.

We want to do the right thing while also minimizing the personal sacrifices or suffering that might entail.

If you, your organization, or other key leaders have failed in a serious ethical obligation, there are many commonsense things you can (and should) do to plan how to manage events and make things right in the aftermath.

However, the act of disclosure always requires an element of faith.

That last step toward laying down the burden will require a deep-seated moral conviction and commitment to the truth that is bigger than yourself.

Lay it down. Offer it up. And trust that, regardless of what happens next, the truth always wins in the end.

HORSESHOES AND HAND GRENADES

Sometimes doing something "close" to right isn't good enough. As a father of four, I find myself increasingly making use of dad-sayings that I learned from my own father when discussing life's most important matters with my children and others.

Mind you, when these pearls of wisdom were dispensed to me as a young man, I rolled my eyes, scoffed, or otherwise convinced myself that my father's sage advice somehow didn't apply to me. We all think our own ethical dilemmas are special, especially when we are teenagers.

If my dad asked me how I did with some critical task, especially one involving doing the right thing where other people were concerned, I frequently hedged by saying that I did the task mostly right or "close" to expectations. The response to this was invariably, "Close only counts in horseshoes and hand grenades." My father was teaching me that there are some tasks and responsibilities that we have a responsibility to do completely, and to the best of our ability, correctly and with precision.

My professional work revolves around interpersonal relationships—building, optimizing, maintaining, and repairing them. It's very rewarding and demanding work. It's also very flexible. There are often multiple right ways to solve an interpersonal problem, and sometimes it can be good enough to get a solution to a relational problem mostly right.

In interpersonal work, consequences resulting from a lack of perfect practice are usually fairly low. Except when they're not. For example, the #MeToo crisis, clergy abuse scandals that rocked the Catholic Church, and the constant drumbeat of teacher/student sex scandals in the K–12 public education world all have one thing in common. In most individual cases, someone knew.

People, often powerful people, knew what was happening and either looked the other way or helped to hide what happened. In the worst cases, they abetted the behavior in order to protect their own careers or ingratiate themselves with the perpetrators.

Leadership is an inherently interpersonal endeavor. It can be a very nuanced and creative art. However, some leadership challenges demand precision and completeness. When it comes to protecting the vulnerable and upholding core ethical and moral principles, close to right isn't good enough.

Everyone enjoys a great office, flashy title, and the leather chair at the end of the big table. However, to whom much is given, much is required. If you stay in a position of leadership long enough, the bill for these privileges will come due. You will be confronted with the choice of whether to do the hard and precise thing or the easy and obfuscating thing.

A top banking executive from Mexico once told me why corruption in the financial system was so difficult to uproot. He said that the problem wasn't knowing what was happening. Many people in his system know at least some of the who and how of the rot.

The real problem, he said, is that everyone feels a little dirty. Everyone feels a little dirty because even the "good" people knew or saw something in the past. It might have been only one instance or a small accounting detail that they knew was a problem—and they did nothing. The moment came to do the right thing, and they balked. They took the easy route and let it go.

This person usually feels deeply guilty. They might feel like a coward. Perhaps they rationalize their inaction by telling themselves that it's not their problem or responsibility, that some other official or entity should act. But at the end of the day, they know that they already ignored the corruption once. It will be easier to ignore it again in the future.

Ultimately, it's not the will of bad people that maintains the corruption but the shame of good people.

We all want to be heroes. We want to believe that when our moment comes, or comes again, we will do the right thing. We hope we will choose to suffer the slings and arrows we know might come. However, the hard reality is that unless we are doing the right thing today, we are very unlikely to do it tomorrow.

Everyone reading this, myself included, has failed in a moral obligation at some point. Perhaps you corrected that failure. Maybe you didn't. Regardless, the only thing each of us controls is what we will do from this day forward.

Here are some queries for self-reflection that I find helpful to keep my ethical compass calibrated and my leadership responsibilities clear:

- Have I seen, heard about, or suspected behavior that raises concerns for the physical or emotional safety of others?
- Have I seen, heard about, or suspected behavior that raises ethical or legal concerns for the health and/or reputation of my organization?
- Have I been pressured to withhold information or willingly kept secrets that should be shared and known?
- Have I done everything in my power to take action and raise this concern directly with those involved and/or with those who have the ability to address the situation?

- If I have failed to raise these concerns directly, what support or assistance do I need to do so? Who specifically can I turn to for help, support, and wise counsel, both inside and outside my organization?
- To what extent am I willing to risk suffering personal consequences for doing the right thing?
- What would help me act more courageously today and in the future?

None of us are perfect. Frequently, we are not as courageous as we could be. However, upholding our core ethics and safeguarding the vulnerable are not horseshoes and hand grenades. Don't let close enough be good enough.

FIGHT TIP

FIND THE QUIET VOICE

In the next section When the Sky Falls, I talk about the lessons that my workplace community learned on 9/11.

One of the key things we did right was that **we gave everyone an opportunity to speak and be heard. We focused on supporting and trying to better understand those around us before taking further action.**

A friend of mine is engaging in similar work right now, helping a religious community grapple with an abuse scandal. As a first step, this community has arranged a few simple forums using practices similar to those described in my 9/11 story. After holding a few of these sessions, my friend shared the most surprising thing that he learned so far.

It's not the great orators, big personalities, or formal leaders that have the biggest impact on the community during these conversations. The most impact is made by the quiet voice—the person who is normally silent but finally has a forum in which to speak.

In my friend's case, it might be the thoughtful person who sits quietly in the back and generally stays out of parish politics and conflict. That person tithes, attends services regularly, and humbly volunteers to help the needy in the community.

When that person finally chooses to speak, people listen.

The next time your workplace community needs to grapple with an important issue, question, or crisis, make sure your conversation is structured to find and hear the quiet voice.

WHEN THE SKY FALLS

On September 11, 2001, I was working as a counselor for at-risk youth at a private school in southeastern Pennsylvania, about an hour and a half from Manhattan.

We had a typical morning gathering with our students. We held a circle. Staff and students did a short "check-in," saying something about how they were feeling that morning. We discussed some goals for the week; then everyone went off to class.

Around 8:45 EDT, like everyone else around the world that day, we realized that something terrible was happening. This was before the era of smartphones. Teachers and staff who were in the habit of playing the radio during class, like the shop and art teachers, were the first to hear what was happening.

I started seeing staff walking down the hall looking odd and shocked. My first thought was to wonder who was absent that day. Our school had many students struggling with drug addiction and trying to break away from various kinds of criminal behavior. Was one of them hurt? Did someone overdose? A quick meeting was called in the counselor's office.

The first plane had just hit the North Tower. Initially, we all assumed it was a terrible accident. Many of our students were from New York and had family living in the city, but we still decided to do nothing yet. We would wait until more information was available.

Then the next plane hit the South Tower. Then the Pentagon was hit. Then another plane crashed in western Pennsylvania. What the hell was happening? The staff were bewildered. Nothing like this had happened in most of our lifetimes. We didn't have a template or script for what to do next. Our responsibilities that day paled in significance compared to the horrors that victims and first responders faced, but we felt overwhelmed.

We were momentarily paralyzed. Eventually, we realized that regardless of how we were feeling, it was wrong to withhold the information from staff and students any longer.

The most interpersonally savvy young people were already starting to ask if something had happened. They could see that the adults were upset. Just like my first reaction, they assumed a classmate was hurt or in trouble.

Not knowing what else to do, we did this. We called another circle in our main meeting room. First, we told them everything we knew. We also told them everything we didn't know. We assured them that as far as we knew, our local area was in no immediate danger. Our school was in a town of no great importance, but still . . . no one really understood what was happening yet.

Next, we said that we would go around the circle, in order and one by one. We used something called a talking-piece, a small object that we passed from person to person. Whoever had the talking-piece was the only one who could talk. The others would listen. We told the group that they could say whatever they needed to say. We asked only that each person speak for themselves and their own feelings, not for others.

There was a kaleidoscope of reactions. Some people just cried. Others were consumed with worry for loved ones in the city. Some staff and students prayed for peace. Others hoped for vengeance against whoever did this to us. There was sadness, worry, anger, and rage. There was wisdom, as well as the natural urge to strike back. In that circle, we began to see the outlines of the new normal, and the new divisions, that would come to define the era we live in today.

Before becoming a counselor, I attended a private military academy. In my undergraduate studies during the early 1990s, I was enrolled in a specialized intensive Russian language program. I was also dual majoring in political science. My classmates and I were preparing to fight the great war of the late twentieth century: the Cold War.

I had a photo negative experience of 9/11 in December of 1991. I was sitting in the cadet lounge with friends. The television was on. The room suddenly erupted into cheers, high-fives, and chest thumping. The news had just broken on CNN that the Soviet Union had fallen.

The "evil empire" was no more. The fall of the Iron Curtain was especially great news for Eastern Europe and millions around the world living under the yoke of murderous communist rule. And yet, those of us in the Russian language department, most of whom were preparing for careers in intelligence and foreign service, were also a bit disoriented. Our war had ended before we even had a chance to join in the battle.

As with 9/11, few people saw this massive change coming in December of 1991. The axis of history turns on such days. Countless individual lives would veer onto a new path. My life's path changed that day as well.

While sitting in the circle with my students on 9/11, I tried to organize a jumble of emotions and thoughts. At that point, it was fairly clear that the attacks were committed by terrorists.

Then and in the days that followed, I couldn't shake the odd memory of going to see the movie Rambo III with my brother as a kid in the summer of '88, when the Cold War still seemed interminable.

In that movie, Sylvester Stallone teams up with the mujahideen in Afghanistan to fight the evil Soviets. In the film, the mujahideen are portrayed as sympathetic heroes driven by a righteous cause to expel a foreign invader. Fast forward to 9/11 and the same people were flying planes into American buildings. That inconsistency and many other inconvenient facts from another era were going down the Orwellian memory hole. We had a new enemy. The new orthodoxy implied that they had always been our enemy. As Orwell's Big Brother had asserted in the book 1984, "We have always been at war with Eurasia." All memories to the contrary were old-think.

With the formal end of the Cold War in 1991, my classmates and I assumed that we would finally enter a long period of peace. That was not to be. A new enemy was ready in the wings. WWI led to WWII. WWII led to the Cold War. The Cold War would lead to the War on Terror.

Now I understood why, after the fall of the Soviet Union, a well-connected faculty member from the Russian department had recommended that I start studying Farsi. "Why would I study Farsi?" I asked at the time. The response was, "Because all of the action will be in the Middle East over the next few decades."

Just like that, one villain was substituted with another. It was clear that there would be no post-Soviet demobilization or "peace dividend." It seemed that our betters had decided that, as the world's lone hyperpower, we had an empire to run. That very day is when I began to morally part ways with the direction of the elites driving US foreign policy. I signed up to defend the defenseless, not build a new imperium that I found morally bankrupt and strategically doomed. And with the disastrous evacuation of Afghanistan, I—and we—now find ourselves with post-Soviet Russia as a purposely recycled enemy for the twenty-first century. It seems our elites can't live without a villain to justify their ambitions. They also seem to be running out of creative talent in fabricating new ones. But I digress. These are conversations for another book.

In the circle with my colleagues and students on 9/11, I doubt anyone would have been interested in my geopolitical disorientation or my own complicated relationship with the country I love. It was a time for raw emotion and relational solidarity, not for intellectual investigation.

When it was my turn to speak, I simply said that my heart ached for those who were dying and suffering. I obliquely shared my other concerns by saying that I feared that many more people were going to die in the coming years. I knew enough about international politics to understand what would soon be unleashed. Many of my family members and old classmates would be going off to a new war. I had no doubt about that.

One of the things I valued most about that day was that I worked in a place, and at a time, when it was understood that there would be a range of emotional reactions and political opinions in the room. We may have shaken our fists at the sky on 9/11, but unlike much of US society today, we didn't shake them at each other. It was the end of a less divided time and the beginning of a far more complicated period of US history. In many situations that followed, I fell back on the lessons from that day and what we did right as a workplace community. First, we told the truth as far as we understood it. Next, we let everyone be heard. Lastly, we focused on supporting and trying to better understand those around us before taking further action.

Each of us was allowed the time to speak. No one was silenced. No one was bullied into ideological agreement or emotional congruence. We made it clear that in this moment, there was no one right way to feel, think, or react.

As I've learned many times in my career, conflict is natural. There's a time to fight. However, conflict is fruitful only when it is matched with a commitment to truth, wisdom, and understanding. These lessons have helped me to assist others when the proverbial sky falls—after a school shooting, criminal malfeasance, workplace betrayals, and professional moral failures, as well as after relational fallings-out in my own life.

In each case, the key factor in organizational and personal recovery was not the depth of the harm or the severity of the event. The key factor was whether the workplace community could still offer care and support to one another despite their differences in personal history, experience, and opinion. Because when the sky falls, we cannot survive alone.

HOW TO FIGHT A WITCH HUNT

Halloween is the one holiday that officially celebrates the things that freak us out. It's a tradition that reaches far back into history and the human psyche. Perhaps like me, during this season in school you were forcibly compelled to read the witchy American novel *The Crucible*, which follows the dark history of the Salem witch trials.

Interestingly, the focus of Arthur Miller's classic masterpiece isn't really witches. It is something far more frightening: the witch hunt. Throughout history, more destruction has been wrought by witch hunts themselves than by any double, double, toil, and trouble cooked up by fanciful witches.

Miller's novel chronicles the seventeenth-century witch trials of Salem, Massachusetts, in which more than two hundred people were accused of witchcraft, and nineteen (fourteen women and five men) were executed. This dark episode in US history is usually remembered as a cautionary tale against superstition and social hysteria.

Apparently, it's also a cautionary tale about mixing LSD-mimicking funguses with a fundamentalist theocracy. Seriously, check this out. It seems that Puritanism was a bad trip on many levels. But history shows that there was something far deeper going on beneath the surface.

Many in the Massachusetts colony were certainly consumed with fear of the diabolical, but the witch trials were also a cynical exercise of power. Old scores were settled. Land from executed "witches" was conveniently confiscated. The ruling caste of the small colony used the process of the trials, and its physical and psychological terrors, to reinforce their position and power.

The supposed threat posed by an arcane spell cast in the forest is rather remote. The threat posed by an irrational mob at one's door with torches is more direct.

In part, Miller wrote *The Crucible* as an allegory for 1950s McCarthyism. However, the deeper warning of this tale is that all communities carry within them a dark potential to become so fundamentalist in their beliefs, whether religious or ideological, that any perceived digression is viewed as an existential threat.

This dynamic unleashes the irrational fears and ruthlessness hiding in the darkest parts of every human heart. As in early Massachusetts, it also provides an opportunity for the worst type of leaders to harness the crisis for their own cynical ends. Workplaces are not immune.

If you look up from your cubicle one day and see a gathering collection of pitchforks and torches, here are some things you need to understand about witch hunts.

Witch hunts are not about finding witches. Instead, the purpose of a witch hunt is to reinforce the power of those who get to do the hunting. One sure sign of a witch hunt is that normal rules for evidence and defense are relaxed or eliminated entirely. Sometimes farcical new methods of gauging guilt are developed for these "special circumstances" that subvert longstanding procedures that would otherwise provide more protection to the accused.

The typical argument is that the threat posed by the supposed witches is so unique, insidious, complicated, and hidden that the old and stuffy ways of justice simply won't do. Evidence, schmevidence. Let's start gathering fire-wood for the pyre. You get the picture.

Witch hunts will expand. When established procedure and norma-tive social behavior are no longer expected, onlookers and bystanders will seek protection from being targeted. This is most easily accomplished by joining in and becoming an accuser as well.

After all, who wants angry villagers at their own door? Now that anyone might be accused with little opportunity for reasonable defense, it's better to be holding a torch than standing on top of the bonfire. This drives all witch hunts into expansion as the number of accusers proliferates and the need to supply new witches increases exponentially.

Opposition to the witch hunt will be portrayed as a sign of collaboration or guilt. Those brave few who refuse to join in the hunt and who speak out against what's happening will likely be accused or impli-cated as collaborators.

This vicious cycle of circular logic reduces the community to a binary. Increasingly, there are only two available groups: the accusers and the guilty. This is another sure sign that a witch hunt is underway. The dynamic serves to silence and cow those leaders and others best placed to help the commu-nity self-correct in the hunt's early stages. It is then that courageous leaders must demand a focus on process first, as the surest means to establishing any legitimate level of guilt or culpability of supposed wrongdoers.

Witch hunts eventually consume themselves. Eventually, in witch hunt economics, demand for witches always outstrips supply. As more and more of the fearful join the witch hunt leaders, eventually there's just not enough alleged witches to go around.

After the marginalized, outliers, and other social or ideological outcasts with the least recourse to self-defense have been consumed, the hunters will begin to turn on one another. This is when things get really weird. The ac-cusations get more fantastical and the targets less believable.

Prior witch hunt collaborators now begin to attack each other. As fervor for the hunt begins to wane, leadership fractures. Typically, the most ex-treme leaders will accuse the more reasonable ones of "going soft" or outright collaboration with the supposed wrongdoers.

As the farce begins to be exposed, those who joined in mostly out of self-preservation begin to fall away. Next, some of the true believers become disillusioned. Some of them fall away as well. Soon, all that's left are the most extreme and cynical hunters. Without the insulation of the larger crowd, the ugliness of the whole affair is increasingly laid bare. There's likely to be more thrashing about at that point, but it's the beginning of the end for the hunt.

How do you fight a witch hunt? Well, it's not easy. If you are the explicit target, it's unlikely that you'll emerge unscathed. However, you can be prepared to survive in the long run. Here are a few tips.

Stay cool *and* fight back. Staying cool is hard when you're being treated unfairly and are under attack. As discussed above, there is always an element of irrationality to a witch hunt.

In the face of an angry mob, it is very tempting to fight fire with fire. However, that is typically ineffective. The hunt is already running on a high-octane combination of extreme emotion and vindictive animus. You'd simply be providing more fuel. Instead, fight fire with ice.

Hold up a mirror to the hunters. Do your best to exhibit the character, stability, and principles so absent in the witch hunters. Remind them and the onlookers of their better selves. Be the active example of a higher standard of behavior. It might not seem like it at first, but others will notice. At this point, your own behavior is one of the few things that you can actually control. Hard as it is, admirable behavior on your part is what's most likely to help others find the courage to speak out against what's happening.

If you do so, the hunt will typically continue to escalate in hopes of goading you into an emotional reaction that will then be twisted as more evidence of your guilt. The hunters want and expect that reaction. Don't give it to them. This is one of the most fundamental ways you can fight back. The contrast between your measured and reasonable behavior and their escalating irrationality will begin to operate as a defense unto itself. This encourages support from those you will need to eventually end the hunt.

Never apologize for something that you didn't do or isn't true. If you are faced with wild or distorted accusations that are simply untrue, it is tempting to admit to something in hopes that it will make this all go away—especially in the early stages of the conflict. If you have done nothing wrong or your actions have been grossly distorted, do not admit or imply false guilt in hopes of placating a mob hungry for someone to punish. It never works and will be considered tantamount to a full confession.

Frequently, a witch hunt will focus on small transgressions or mistakes but then magnify them to diabolical proportions. You will be encouraged to admit to the small or unintentional error but then be punished as if it is an intentional capital crime. Understand, regardless of what's offered, there are no plea deals in a witch hunt.

One of the most toxic aspects of a witch hunt is that they tend to invert the normal rules of justice. They formally or informally imply a presumption of guilt rather than innocence. The problem with this is that it is simply impossible to prove a negative—to prove that something *didn't* happen. That's why most modern justice systems presume innocence and place the onus on the prosecution to produce credible evidence of guilt.

For instance, if I accuse someone of kicking a puppy over the weekend, how could they prove that they did not? They might try to account for their time over the weekend, who they were with, or try to show that they otherwise had no opportunity to kick a puppy. But I might respond that surely there still must have been some time when you might have had an opportunity to kick a puppy. How are we to know? After all, puppy-kickers are probably very crafty people, and so on.

To the extent possible, leave the burden of proof with those making the accusation. The same rule applies whether the accusation comes through formal channels, or more typically, through informal social networks and relationships. If evidence is presented, respond to it as needed. Otherwise, don't do their work for them. Never work harder than the hunters.

Focus on the long run. I'm sorry to tell you this, but if you are the target of a true witch hunt, you are going to take damage in the short term. It's unavoidable. Witch hunt dynamics empower the unscrupulous for precisely this reason: the hunt provides an opportunity to do maximal damage with the lowest possible threshold of proof and behavioral standards.

Even if the witch hunt is initially spawned by a truly righteous cause, the allure of easy power typically brings the worst kind of leaders to the fore. The rest are then either corrupted, silenced, or turned into targets themselves. Accusations, even if eventually proved to be untrue or not credible, will harm you. Just as in politics, casual observers will remember the accusation not the retraction—especially if the charge is something they wanted to be true in the first place.

Fighting a witch hunt is not really about winning. It's more about surviving in the long term by being consistent, truthful, and resilient. Steel yourself for a marathon. This will not be over soon. It will be painful. Staying cool and guarding your own self-respect by maintaining high standards for your own behavior will give you the endurance advantage. You will get stronger as others burn themselves out.

Be a hard target and stand up for the vulnerable. Another great irony of a witch hunt is that, although they present a fearsome spectacle, they typically target people who are already perceived as weakened, compromised, or marginalized in some way. The Salem witch trials began by targeting elderly single women, a slave, and children.

The first targets are usually those who will have the most difficulty fighting back or whom the larger community already views as suspect or as outsiders. Only later do witch hunts typically seek more difficult targets as demand for witches outstrips supply. The more you are generally seen as someone who stays cool, fights back, cannot be pressured into false apologies, and is willing to stick it out to the end, you will become a hard target. The typical witch hunt will usually look elsewhere for easier quarry.

If you are already a hard target, consider your responsibility to stand up for those more vulnerable than you. It is not only morally right but also strategically smart to defend the innocent who might be in a weaker position. Soberly consider the wisdom of Aleksandr I. Solzhenitsyn: "The simple step of a courageous individual is not to take part in the lie."

After all, once successful and emboldened, the hunters might eventually come for you.

Witch hunt dynamics are always inherently destructive, no matter the target or the cause they support. This is especially true if real harms have occurred. Illegitimate process undermines legitimate claims. Witch hunts further undermine the pursuit of real justice as the hunt devolves into a cynical bid for power instead of a sincere effort to reveal, acknowledge, and repair harm.

FIGHT TIP

SCHEDULE A CONVERSATION WITH A HERETIC

The section How to Fight a Witch Hunt covered how to fight back if you find angry villagers, torches, and pitchforks at your door. **All communities and organizations carry within them a dark potential to become so fundamentalist in their beliefs or culture that any perceived digression is viewed as an existential threat.**

That fear is what usually spawns a witch hunt in the first place. What can leaders do to make that devilish dynamic less likely? Here's one suggestion:

Schedule a conversation with a heretic.

Deeply and honestly reflect on who in your organization most disagrees with you. Who sees the world through an entirely different lens? Who do you suspect is operating from a fundamentally different range of assumptions about people, the world, or the vision for your work? We normally avoid those people. Don't.

A conversation does not require that you come to a negotiated agreement on how you see the world. However, a real conversation will help ensure that you understand the people around you.

Don't debate. Don't present opposing ideas. Just ask questions. Then listen.

Give the other person confidence that you are genuinely curious about how they see things and only want to understand them more fully. Especially if that person tends toward rigidity in their own thinking, this is an opportunity to demonstrate openness to other ways of seeing the world and comfort in the face of disagreement.

Complete agreement, whether on personal or professional matters, is not necessary for a productive relation-

ship. Workplaces that formally or informally demand such agreement are the ones that spawn witch hunts.

Some ideas are inherently in opposition and cannot be easily reconciled—or perhaps not reconciled at all. In those cases, it's doubly important that the relationship is one grounded in a deep understanding of one another. Otherwise, things will tend to arc toward fear and misunderstanding.

Go find a heretic. You might learn something unexpected.

With this in mind, organizational leaders have a grave responsibility to maintain the integrity of legitimate avenues for redress and reparation, whether formal or informal—so that the real needs of those harmed are not lost in the chaos of mob justice and organizational dysfunction.

All human communities, whether in the workplace or civil society, have the potential to turn upon themselves and give breathing room to unjust persecution. For the historically minded, check out Milton Mayer's chilling account of 1940s Germany in the book They Thought They Were Free about how otherwise ordinary people can come to persecute their friends and neighbors.

I have seen several versions of the witch hunt run their course through organizations. There will come a time at the very end of a witch hunt when those left standing in the relational rubble will look at one another and ask, "My goodness, what have we done?" When that time comes, the community always looks for answers from trusted leaders whose principles and integrity are still intact. Hopefully, we are all working hard to be that kind of leader.

TOXIC WORKPLACE BEHAVIOR PROFILE

THE ASTRONAUT

Code Name: The Astronaut
Motto: Get off my cloud!
Favorite Song: "Spaceman" by 4 Non Blondes
Favorite Movie: *The Martian*
Behavior: A business professor of mine once told me a story about working at a major international tech company during the heyday of the still-new computer industry in the '60s and '70s. This was a time when some of the brightest minds in tech were still designing computers without much help from . . . computers.

That meant that coders and engineers were doing lots of new and complicated mathematical work longhand. No AI assistance was available. Much of the coding work still involved chalk on boards and ink on paper. The calculations and tests that could be run produced reams upon reams of paper printouts even for the simplest of functions.

Finding an error required long painstaking work reviewing miles of code using the most powerful computer in existence at the time: the human brain. The company had a small army of the best mathematicians, drawn from leading universities around the world, collaborating on these crucial binary puzzles from the dawn of computing. However, there was one guy who worked entirely alone. Always.

While everyone else showed up to work in short-sleeve dress shirts, pocket protectors, and slacks, this guy wore dingy cut-off jean shorts, flip flops, and was famous for his poor and somewhat offensive hygiene. He didn't graduate from an impressive school. In fact, as I recall, he hadn't graduated from any school—either because he dropped out or was never interested. He was . . . their Astronaut.

He wasn't literally a space explorer. However, he was a singular individual who lived alone in the outer reaches of the company—mentally as well as physically. He was unwilling or unable to integrate into the regular life and culture of the organization. Few people knew how he passed his time. Word was that he largely snacked and watched television in his little windowless room most days. Apparently, he was also well paid to do so. Why?

Well, there were times when an entire team of brilliant computer engineers could not fix or find an error in a mountain of code. In those rare cases, they would deliver a wheelbarrow of data (on actual paper) to him. Most times he would simply scan it with his eyes for a few moments, pause, cock his head to the side, and point. "Here," he would say, identifying a microscopic bit of code. He'd then go back to his sandwich and watching cartoons.

Without fail, when the engineers checked what he had identified, they would realize that, yet again, their Astronaut had discovered the error. In mere moments, he could find a mistake that a whole team hadn't been able to pinpoint in days or weeks of troubleshooting. Their Astronaut was beyond genius. He was a true mathematical and machine-language savant.

You might ask, why did the company only deploy his abilities occasionally? Why wasn't this mental giant leading the entire division? The problem was that the Astronaut lacked the ability and/or desire to relate to others. True, he was fantastically gifted but only within a narrow bandwidth of human activity. Successful companies are not built by superstars; they are built by teams.

There are rare cases like this one, when an Astronaut can find a small valuable niche in the life of an organization. However, in the majority of cases there is more long-term value in finding bright and motivated people who might not be savant-level performers but who know (or can be taught) how to relate and collaborate with others.

Do Not: Do not punish brilliance or socially ostracize outlier high performers. Some organizations are so committed to the "team mentality" that they disincentivize the surfacing of genius in their staff.

Each of us has equal inherent value, but humans are not innately equal in all areas of talent and ability. Avoid the misconception that being a team means being the same. Mutually reinforced mediocrity helps no one. However, when faced with a stellar talent who is having difficulty integrating into the relational life of the organization, you have some decisions to make.

Do: First, if the Astronaut is knowingly and consciously leveraging their abilities to create their own special rules, norms, privileges, and favors, that must stop. Never let your organization be held hostage by outlier top performers. The long-term benefits of a healthy culture always outweigh the short-terms gains offered by singular brilliance.

It is also possible, as in the previous example, that the Astronaut is so talented that they truly have difficulty relating to people, through no real fault of their own. Actual geniuses and practical savants are far more likely to be drawn toward solitary work rather than team-based collaboration. They need time and space to run at their true full speed. However, that doesn't mean they get to run roughshod over others.

As a leader, don't allow someone's exceptional smarts to let them off the hook for learning how to work effectively with others. While others can admire the Astronaut's talents, the Astronaut should be humble, admiring the ability of others to collaborate effectively and learning from them. Not everyone can be a genius, but everyone needs to learn how to work together.

Lastly, don't overestimate the value of outlier performers and Astronauts. If your organization has a few that have managed to integrate into the organizational culture, that's great. Count your lucky stars and treat those people well. However, avoid cults of intelligence as much as cults of personality, and trust that grit almost always beats innate talent in the long run—personally and in team-based work. As a leader, I'll take a committed group of gritty, dedicated professionals over a loosely connected gaggle of Divas and Astronauts every single time. The biggest battles in life and in an organization don't require genius. They require guts, fortitude, and a rock-solid commitment to the success and welfare of the people standing next to you.

And if you happen to be the rare Astronaut, remember, no one gets to the Moon alone.

PRINCIPLE 9:
LEAD FROM THE FUTURE

Ask a child to complete a maze in an activity book. If they are the savvy sort, they will likely begin at the part marked "end" and not at the place marked "start." Through direct experience, children learn that it's easier to complete a maze successfully when you do it in reverse.

This was a recent lesson from a strategic planning mentor that helped my organization dream bigger. Like a child staring at a maze, when an organization has a vision for how it wants to expand, evolve, or level up, there's usually a spaghetti plate of twisting routes between "where we are now" and "where we want to be."

In this early stage of change, leaders face the dual challenge of too many options and lots of potential dead ends. Leaders that like a challenge and dislike uncertainty will tend to plunge ahead and trace their path by instinct. That feels bold and exciting, but you typically wind up with a lot of tracing, erasing, and retracing of paths through the labyrinth of change.

You're also likely to become myopically focused on overcoming the immediate obstacles in front of your face and lose sight of whether your overall direction is taking you toward the intended destination. A wilderness survival expert once told me, "As soon as you even suspect you're getting lost, go back to the last waypoint where you knew your precise location." This is sound advice for life as well as managing change in an organization.

It's a simple instruction. However, ego will conspire to drive most people forward anyway. They will tell themselves, "When I top that ridge, make it out of this valley, or find that lake, I'll know where I am. I'm not really lost." All the while, they move deeper and deeper into unknown terrain until they lose their bearings completely. They might make it out, but they're unlikely to arrive at the destination they intended.

It takes discipline to stop, think, and act strategically. It also takes humility. Children are often much better at mazes than adults. They have less ego. Children assume that mazes are hard. They don't feel pressure (like adults do) to make the task look easy. So, they're more likely to think it through first and look for an advantage—like starting from the desired endpoint and working backward.

Children also know that there are traps built into every maze and take those traps seriously. However, those traps are really designed for those working from start to finish. When you work from the end backward to the starting point, you bypass most of the dead ends, distractions, and paths to nowhere. Consultants get paid lots of money to reteach this strategic planning truth to leaders. It's also true when leading conflict and changing relationships.

Principle 9, Lead from the Future, means this:

When seeking to transform a relationship with a difficult colleague or shift the culture in your organization, behave as if the thing you want to be true has already happened. Then work backward to fill in the relational or cultural architecture that will cement that reality into place.

Let's say staff behavior is rife with mistrust and gossip. You have a vision for a new organizational culture that is frank and transparent, while also being kind and understanding. The problem is, when you start from the beginning and plunge ahead, every move you make toward that new culture will be obstructed by the very behavioral habits you want to change—just like the traps in a maze.

The way to work the maze backward is to immediately begin to behave as if the cultural and/or relational change you seek has already happened. In other words, become the outlier that is first to embody and model the future behavior change you seek in others, while simultaneously treating unwanted behavior that has been the norm as the aberration.

When practiced consistently, this immediately resets the baseline of what is considered normal behavior in the relationship or organizational culture. When a leadership team does this in unison, change happens rapidly.

In the example where mistrust and gossip have been the norm in the organization, you would "start from the end" by strenuously and publicly modeling the opposite healthy behaviors you want to see in others, even if you need to fake it until you make it. Ensure that your modeling stands out and is noticed. You will feel alone at first. It will feel weird. After all, you're disrupting fixed patterns of behavior.

Even if existing patterns are unhealthy, people are used to things being that way. "Bad" is often more comfortable than uncertain. Additionally, new instances of gossip and untrustworthy behavior should be met with shock and strong immediate disapproval. Instead of responding with statements like, "I know this has always been a gossipy workplace, but we need to change this," the response should be, "The amount of gossiping here is shocking to me.

This is not who we are as an organization. It's harmful, and no one should tolerate it."

The first response rightly points out the problem (i.e., the gossipy culture) but implies that someone else, at some undefined point in the future, needs to change that behavior. In a workplace already marked by mistrust, good luck waiting for someone else to take the first risk if you're not willing to do it yourself as a leader. Calling out a problem is the easy part. Being the first person to embody the alternative behavior is the hard part.

The second response (i.e., leading from the future) not only rejects the unwanted behavior, it also actively models the desired new behavior and immediately sets a new expectation for what will be considered normal.

At first, you will be inhabiting a future populated by only one person, you. Starting to lead in this new way may leave most people in the organization feeling puzzled or disoriented. Some will be thinking, "What is he talking about? Gossipy and mistrustful is exactly who we are! It's always been like this."

Over time, though, others will join you. This happens slowly at first. However, once enough numbers have been accumulated to provide a feeling of safety to the reticent, culture can shift quite quickly.

This works the same way with any shift. Maybe your organization's mission is evolving. Perhaps you want a new R&D team to move from a fixed to a growth mindset. Or you just want people to start cleaning up after themselves in the break room. Whatever that shift is for your team, it's far more likely to happen when the leader starts from the end of the maze, stands in the future where the change has already happened, and says, "Join me."

LEAD CONFLICT LIKE THE GOAT

To most boxing fans, Muhammad Ali is the undisputed GOAT (greatest of all time). For sure, he was a great boxer. But he won most of his fights before he even stepped into the ring.

Ali was a master of the psychology of conflict as much as he was an expert boxer. For Ali, the real fight began long before the first-round bell. He was always several steps ahead of his opponents, mentally as well as physically.

For some personal and in-depth reflections on what it was like to face Ali inside and outside the ring, check out the documentary Facing Ali. This film interviews some of the most famous, and toughest, boxers of the twentieth century. Each one recounts the multitude of ways Ali beat them psychologically before he beat them physically. All of Ali's famous jawing at the camera and boasting was a strategy, not just ego. The fight had already started, but Ali was the only one punching—metaphorically speaking.

I'm not suggesting you trash-talk like Ali in your next team meeting. Although, that would be hilarious. Be sure to Instagram that. (Then dust off your résumé. You'll likely be looking for a new job!) However, I am suggesting that you lead conflict at work by getting far ahead of those you lead, especially regarding natural team friction and toxic personalities. You need to know where you want team relationships to be in the future and start making the moves in the present to get them there.

Most creative conflicts and toxic personality issues are entirely predictable once you stop avoiding interpersonal engagement and start consistently moving toward it—toward the fear. When you can predict the behavior of others and are willing to engage early, you can more easily drive the conflict where you want it to go.

Perhaps the best example of this is Muhammad Ali and George Foreman's famous "Rumble in the Jungle" fight in Zaire (now the Democratic Republic of the Congo) in 1974. In the lead-up to the fight, Ali used every skill and resource at his disposal to defeat a younger, ferocious, and much feared George Foreman. Ali used the following four principles to succeed, and so should you.

1. Have a plan to "win."

Except in the rare case of a draw, winning and losing in boxing is zero sum. One boxer will have their arm raised in victory at the end of the bout. But Ali didn't just expect to win, he planned to win. He had a clear vision of the path to victory in this specific situation and understood the particular challenges presented by George Foreman as a boxer. Winning the actual boxing match was just the last step. The really hard and creative work was done before he stepped into the ring.

Unlike the friendly, grill-selling grandpa we all know from television commercials, George Foreman was known as an intimidating power-puncher back in the day. He was a bully in the ring and relied on his ability to inspire fear in his opponents, then crush them with power shots. If Ali was a nimble sports car, Foreman was a crushing bulldozer.

To lead conflict, you must plan rather than simply react. When done for the right reasons and intentions, this is not manipulation. Transformative leaders, problem solvers, and creative team members are excellent at "reading" a group and guiding their activity intentionally. This begins with devoting sufficient time to plan how, when, and where you will influence these relationships and key stakeholders.

Everything Ali did in Zaire, from the moment he stepped off the plane to the moment his hand was raised in victory, was part of a plan.

2. Harness the power of the crowd.

In the press and in public, Ali played the inspirational populist. The people of Zaire identified with him. They loved Ali. He became a folk hero. In contrast, Foreman came off as a brooding and humorless bully. Eventually, he would be jeered during public appearances. Foreman got beat in the ring, but first he was slaughtered in the battle of hearts and minds.

A tribal religious leader even supposedly put a curse on Foreman! It's unclear whether this ever actually happened, but the Ali camp encouraged the story, knowing that Foreman was deeply superstitious. Even Foreman later admitted that he wondered if Ali's victory would be inevitable because of the supposed curse.

All this worked for Ali because the strategy was based in truth (OK, except for the curse). Ali was likable. Foreman was aloof and broody. Ali simply amplified and contrasted things that were true and leveraged them to his own advantage. While Foreman trained privately and with grim determination, Ali worked the public with his endlessly expansive personality and charisma. No one, even an ultimate tough guy like Foreman, likes feeling like the afterthought at the party.

Foreman reflected later how draining this was for him. To have a country of millions universally and passionately rooting for your opponent tends to get into your head. By the time the first bell rang, it felt like the whole world was rooting for Ali. Foreman showed up angry, anxious, and doubtful—not a winning combo in boxing.

When you lead conflict, avoid tunnel vision. Take a wide view on strategy. The conflict is not about one person, meeting, or challenge. The conflict involves every relationship in the team and a longer timeline within which to work than you may appreciate at first. Remember, the goal is to win before you get into the ring, not after.

There is truly an ocean of relational resources available to you, even in a small team. Everyone can play a role in leading a conflict where you want it to go. Be creative and expansive in your thinking about when, how, and where to leverage these resources.

3. Loosen the ropes.

Foreman showed up angry and tense. Given his brawling and power-punching style, his behavior in the ring was now very predictable—just as Ali intended. Foreman rushed at Ali with an onslaught of destruction. All Ali needed to do was stay on his feet, conserve his energy, and let Foreman tire himself out. Then, once they were in the proverbial deep end of the later rounds, Ali would use his superior speed and mobility to dismantle a bulldozing Foreman, who would be out of gas and emotionally drained. That's exactly what happened.

While Ali was letting Foreman punch himself into exhaustion, Ali would lean far back against the ropes and cover his face to avoid being knocked out. In boxing lore, this is referred to as his "rope-a-dope" strategy. This was so successful, it was widely rumored (but never proven) that the Ali camp had ensured that the ring ropes would be excessively loosened. Hypothetically, this enabled Ali to lean back much farther while on the ropes and avoid the worst of Foreman's onslaught.

I am not recommending you do anything unethical when leading conflict. However, you should see all aspects of your environment as potential advantages. Be strategic in choosing how, when, or in which meeting to raise a concern—including who will, and will not, be there. Time important conversations (or confrontations) smartly and in a way that supports your intended outcomes. Make sure your strategy is more powerful than your impulses.

Talk to people who are likely to support your position before an important meeting or conversation. Tell them you plan to raise a concern. Ask for their support in the meeting. Maybe do this with several people. This isn't cheating. It's leading. Seemingly small details, such as choosing who to sit next to in a meeting or planning who will talk first during a critical presentation, can all have a measurable influence on success. Nothing is ever guaranteed to go as planned. The more variables you can account for and leverage, the better.

4. Be gracious in winning.

In this case, nearly everything went as Ali had planned and hoped. The fight was stopped in the eighth round as an exhausted Foreman was unable to defend himself against arguably the best technical boxer in history.

In the press, Ali continued to be Ali, with his wonderful, over-the-top, and never-ending bravado. Even more than boxing, Ali was a master at being, well, Ali. He flawlessly played his self-crafted persona. It wasn't only ego. It was an intentional strategy.

But privately, Ali and Foreman became great friends. Foreman later emotionally recounted that Ali was his greatest friend and mentor, both inside and outside the ring. He even thanked Ali for helping him learn how to sell his famous "George Foreman Grills." Google those old TV ads. Gone is the brooding Foreman the Boxer. You'll see a warm, charming, and loveable guy. That's a much better persona for selling grills. Foreman credits Ali with teaching him how to be an effective businessman and salesperson. In 1984, Ali was diagnosed with Parkinson's disease and began a long physical and mental decline. Foreman, his mental and physical health amazingly intact, built a business empire—and made far more money selling electric grills than he ever did boxing.

All these tips should be used in the best interest of others, not for mere personal gain, aggrandizement, or just to win. Unlike boxing, zero-sum games are rarely useful in workplace conflict. You need honorable motives to really lead. Ali was a beloved boxer and leader because he was, in fact, truly great. All the flash and stratagems aside, he spent a lifetime perfecting his craft. He also cared deeply about those who looked up to him. The aforementioned strategies worked only because Ali was a superb boxer as well as a compassionate human being.

Similarly, you must commit to building and practicing the skill set you need to lead conflict. Also, you must truly want the best for others if those skills are going to make a positive difference. If your team believes you really want the best for them, they will follow your lead. Like Ali in Zaire, you can't do it alone. You need social capital and the help of others to succeed. Ali was loved and admired, not because of some trick but because he was truly lovable and admirable. Be self-giving and authentic when you lead conflict— while also, like Ali, being who your team needs you to be. And occasionally, if really needed, loosen the ropes.

FIGHT TIP

DO THE HARDEST THING FIRST

In the section Creating a Deliberately Developmental Organization, I share how several hundred staff in an organization I worked for created something we call our "basic concepts."

Our basic concepts express, in the clearest way possible, how everyone in the organization was expected to approach relationships and conflict, with each other and with those we served.

They were:

We believe that people are capable of growing and learning in their work and behavior.

We respond to situations WITH people, not TO them, FOR them, or NOT at all.

We separate the deed from the doer by affirming the worth of the individual while disapproving of inappropriate behavior.

People function best in an environment that encourages free expression of emotion—minimizing the negative and maximizing the positive, but allowing people to say what is really on their minds.

We are not expected to have all the answers. Instead of trying to answer or act without adequate knowledge, we need to ask others for help.

We hold each other accountable by giving and receiving feed¬back respectfully.

We act as role models by admitting when we are wrong and being humble.

We help people develop competencies rather than providing the answers for them.

These were visible and discussed everywhere in the organization. There were posters of them in meeting rooms, common areas, and even in the bathrooms! They were reviewed at the beginning of meetings and discussed deeply in private supervision.

Additionally, each individual was asked to consider which basic concept they struggle with the most and will plan to improve in that area this year—including what support and accountability they will need from others.

These were written by our team and for our team, but the ideas are universal. As you think about creating basic concepts with your own team, consider the following.

Which of the "basic concepts" would you find most challenging? What can you do every day to evolve and grow in that area?

Focusing on strengths is a popular idea these days. However, we still need to step up and face the things we fear and avoid. The people who depend on us deserve it.

A great way to start, and lead from the future, is to do the hardest thing first—sometimes before anyone else steps up.

ARE YOU A GAS PEDAL, STEERING WHEEL, OR BRAKE?

A wise mentor once taught me that every effective team needs three people: a gas pedal, a steering wheel, and a brake. The gas pedal provides the needed energy to push the team into action. At optimal functioning, this is not an act of force or coercion. Instead, the gas pedal has a direct connection with, and brings access to, the fuel that makes any movement possible.

In an organization, the gas pedal translates vision into action—potential into kinetic energy.

The steering wheel excels at keeping an eye on the direction of things. This is more than just keeping the car on the road. The steering wheel ensures that we are all going where we think we are going and by the most efficient route. The steering wheel channels and guides the momentum of things, ensuring that every expenditure of energy is purpose-driven and focused.

Finally, the brake operates as a check on the gas pedal and steering wheel. The brake is risk-conscious and situationally aware. The brake has the power to slow or shut things down in the face of danger and crisis. The brake must be someone courageous enough to challenge the combined influence of the gas pedal and steering wheel, yet humble enough not to constantly grind things to a halt.

As in any tripartite dynamic, the interplay can be complex. However, when functioning at a high level, these roles generate purposeful momentum that is strategic and responsive to external conditions and threats. For instance, this is the balance that venture capital looks for in the leadership of a start-up. Investors don't bet on one individual or idea alone. They bet on teams. This mix is what a would-be founder requires to make a fantastic dream a practical reality. The dance between these three roles is what is needed to turn an early and exciting burst of success into a mature and lasting business.

Surely, we perform each of these functions in different situations as circumstances demand. However, on any high-performing team, you are likely to perform one of these roles more deliberately than the other two. In the team you serve today, which one are you? Here's some advice for each of you:

If you're the gas pedal, the biggest temptation is to get together with the steering wheel and decide to discard the brake. When this happens, velocity increases as your natural check is removed. Unable to slow things down, the steering wheel tries to keep up, assuring you that no matter how fast you go, they can keep the rubber on the road. This inevitably ends with a wreck on the side of the road or running out of fuel in the middle of nowhere. When an organization has a fiery and apocalyptic ending, you can usually thank the gas pedal.

If you're the steering wheel, your biggest temptation will be drawing everyone into a never-ending planning process. You will build intricate designs and multiphased strategies for proverbial bridges to nowhere. The danger here is that organization, measurement, and strategizing become an end unto themselves. Each meeting spawns a rationale for more meetings that cover the entire organization in a web of bureaucracy that grows like an alien fungus. Everyone looks exceptionally busy, but nothing external really happens. An unregulated gas pedal risks catastrophic sudden death. A steering wheel run amok risks suspended animation: sitting at the light, revving the engine, scouring the map, and going nowhere.

If you're the brake, your biggest temptation will be to demand the elimination of all risk and doubt before action is taken. If your cautious and care-taking impulses are left unchecked, you smother the team in concern, challenges, what-abouts, and warnings. This can kill creativity and sap the appetite for either initiative or planning. In other words, everyone is about to die, break things, or embarrass themselves and you are the only thing standing between the team and their plunge into the abyss. If not directly pulling the plug on projects, you'll seek to slow-walk the initiative of the gas pedal, usually by enlisting the planning urges of the steering wheel to ensure the latest "crazy idea" dies in committee. The steering wheel is happy to oblige. Plus, the gas pedal likely has such a short attention span that they'll probably forget which of the fourteen ideas they generated this week were never implemented!

However, when everyone accepts their strengths and weaknesses and develops the humility to defer and listen to their teammates, your team becomes both agile and wise.

CREATING A DELIBERATELY DEVELOPMENTAL ORGANIZATION

As we discussed in Principle 6, Grow in Public, a deliberately developmental culture is only made by cultivating deliberately developmental people. Check out an excellent book on this topic, *An Everyone Culture: Becoming a Deliberately Developmental Organization*, by Robert Kegan and Lisa Laskow Lahey. A deliberately developmental organizational culture persistently pushes team members to the edges of their current competencies. That is, by definition, not a place where most people feel comfortable. Fear, insecurity, and conflict live in that place. It's a reach into the unknown. How do you get your team to go there? The first step is to convince them that no one will be asked to journey alone. You'll go together.

Here's a real-life example from my own experience. Several years ago in a prior company, we engaged the entire organization (a consortium of organizations with staff and other stakeholders based in the US, Canada, Latin America, and Europe) in updating one of the most foundational keystones of our own deliberately developmental culture: our "basic concepts." These basic concepts had existed in one form or another in our organization for more than thirty years. However, we'd experienced a rapid evolution and expansion over the last decade. It was time for a fresh look at our culture. This was a good place to start.

Our basic concepts express, in the clearest way possible, how everyone in the organization is expected to approach relationships—with each other and with those we serve. They govern the formal and informal use of power, provide rules of the road for navigating conflict, and make it clear that personal development is an integral part of working with us.

After more than a year of in-person and online meetings, feedback gathering, and many informal conversations, we developed a new and revised set of basic concepts. We decided on:

- We believe that people are capable of growing and learning in their work and behavior.
- We respond to situations WITH people, not TO them, FOR them, or NOT at all.
- We separate the deed from the doer by affirming the worth of the individual while disapproving of inappropriate behavior.
- People function best in an environment that encourages free expression of emotion—minimizing the negative and maximizing the positive, but allowing people to say what is really on their minds.
- We are not expected to have all the answers. Instead of trying to answer or act without adequate knowledge, we need to ask others for help.
- We hold each other accountable by giving and receiving feed¬back respectfully.
- We act as role models by admitting when we are wrong and being humble.

- We help people develop competencies rather than providing the answers for them.

As you can see from this list, these collective commitments are few in number, easy to understand, and largely behavioral. They apply equally to everyone and all job roles—from the president and the board to the newest intern.

Building a shared commitment to these ideas among several hundred staff was a significant undertaking. Effectively integrating them into our daily work lives required ongoing effort and creativity. Over the following year, all units in the organization spent valuable meeting and team-building time discussing and reinforcing how these commitments informed all that we did. The basic concepts became part of our hiring and onboarding processes. They were not optional. When you joined the team, you committed to abiding by these ideas and behaviors. People could be, and were, let go for habitually and willfully violating them.

On a very practical level, the basic concepts also helped to ensure that our organization was a place that people looked forward to showing up to each day, which is no small feat. As such, this was time well spent. Our basic concepts did not make us perfect people or prevent conflict. In fact, they encouraged creative and productive conflict. As we hiked through the forest of team formation and workplace relationships, they ensured that all our relational compasses were pointed in the same direction. Mission statements are great, but it takes time and deep collective reflection to clarify how that mission should be actualized in lived daily behavior. This was a creative effort to provide that clarity.

What would your organization's "basic concepts" look like? What might you learn about each other through the process of engagement? If you're serious about creating a more explicit and deliberate developmental culture, how much time and mental bandwidth are you willing to devote to making the journey into the developmental unknown a success?

TOXIC WORKPLACE BEHAVIOR PROFILE

THE KOMMISSAR

Code Name: The Kommissar

Motto: May I see your papers, please?

Favorite Song: "Der Kommissar" by After the Fire, and also by another '80s artist, Falco, for some German funk-tastic flavor

Favorite Movie: *The Lives of Others*

Behavior: The Kommissar is similar to the behavior profile of the Puritan. They are both marked by inflexible commitment to some form of dogma. However, there's a key difference. The Puritan is a "true believer" and Kool-Aid drinker par excellence. The toxicity of the Puritan's behavior is rooted in their blind and inflexible, though truly sincere, commitment to a narrow range of ideas or opinions. This might be beliefs about a business process, a view of the marketplace, a worldview beyond your organization's actual mission, or any other area of concern that inspires deeply held beliefs. Puritanic behavior is marked less by what ideas they hold dear and more by the rigid way in which they attempt to promote and protect those ideas from examination and debate.

Deeply held beliefs should indeed inform the work of individuals as they engage a diverse range of colleagues who might see things differently. However, the Puritan's behavior becomes toxic in the extent to which they believe they have the one true way of viewing a critical organizational issue. This leads to black-and-white, with-me-or-against-me, zero-sum thinking and explains why they tend to stifle debate and attack nonconformity as an existential threat.

The Kommissar exercises power and influence by operating as a functionary in the service of some inflexible dogma, belief system, person, or group of people—but for crasser reasons. The Kommissar need not be, and often isn't, a "true believer" in the proper sense. The Puritan is a risk-taker and willing to go out on a limb to pursue big ideas, however toxically they may do so. The Kommissar, conversely, is not a risk-taker. Instead, they are excellent at gauging which way the wind is blowing and then setting their sails accordingly once the coast is clear. Where the Puritan is reckless and zealous, the Kommissar is cautious and opportunistic. The Puritan promotes a narrow band of "right-think." The Kommissar obsessively observes, investigates, and polices nonconformity and "wrong-think." The Kommissar is not promoting their own ideas. Instead, they are gaining advantage over others by enforcing the dictates of another more powerful interest. Sometimes that interest is a superior in the organizational hierarchy, an institutional subculture, or a cultural/political zeitgeist.

This behavior typically emerges only after a Puritan (see Round Two) has made significant cultural headway in an institution: lowering the adoption/risk threshold for others and creating incentives for those willing to promote the coalescing dogma. We can all fall prey to this behavior in one form or another. Here are some other sure signs that we or others might be behaving like a Kommissar.

Habitually speaking *for* others. A Kommissar's influence is often derived from their role as self-appointed representative of some idea or group of people other than themselves. They habitually speak in the amorphous "we," especially when challenging others or attempting to influence the organization beyond their actual scope of responsibility. This serves to insulate them from debate by portraying themselves as a spokesperson for others who are not present. In doing so, the Kommissar implies that they are virtuously speaking for those who cannot speak for themselves.

In reality, the Kommissar purposely positions themselves in this "speaker for" role because it is advantageous to them personally, and not necessarily for the group they claim to represent.

Prioritizing compliance over relationships. A Kommissar's value and power is rooted in their ability to produce conformity in behavior and expression. As such, they are often willing to sacrifice trust and hard-earned social capital in an organization by applying informal group pressure tactics and the threat of social ostracization. This increases compliance and conformity, while degrading relational cohesion.

Pathologizing disagreement. Since compliance is the predetermined goal, and the rightness of the dogma is assumed to be unassailable, those who disagree must either be evil or crazy. Those who disagree are not treated as equals who simply see things differently; they are cast as being dangerous or in some way inherently defective.

This provides an excuse as to why debate and the free exchange of ideas are not required or even to be desired.

Ends justify the means. Here, the Kommissar is most like the Puritan. However, while the Puritan is driven by passion and dreams of utopia, the Kommissar is driven by results and the accumulation of social advantage über alles.

Often the goal is not only to censor others but to create an environment where people will censor themselves for fear of running afoul of the dogma or its adherents. This conformity is paid for with social capital. As such, this behavior is never sustainable as it erodes the relational architecture of an organization. These stultifying cultures strangle freedom of thought and expression—and thus creativity, innovation, and mission-critical self-reflection.

Do Not: Do not enable the Kommissar's assumption of unearned influence and unofficial authority. While a Puritan might need time to come down from their lofty and emotionally addictive ideological perch, a Kommissar often responds best to being pushed. Do not allow them influence in the name of others and beyond the role for which they were hired—at least until they learn to exercise leadership with more honesty, grace, and relational skill.

Do: Insist that the Kommissar speak for themselves and not for others. Instead of "We think . . . ," "people are saying . . . ," and "there are many who . . . ," insist on I-centered statements such as "I think . . . ," "I would like to propose . . . ," and "I want/need . . ."

This will help the Kommissar find their own authentic voice and allow others to speak on their own behalf. Often, those voices have been suppressed (unintentionally or not) by the Kommissar's self-serving effort to protect their role as unofficial "spokesperson."

Actively seek and give space for the voices of those for whom the Kommissar has been presuming to speak. Often, leadership created the opportunity for the Kommissar by legitimately failing to recognize, engage, and listen to key ideas, people, or groups within the organization. In other words, the Kommissar simply took advantage of a deficit that leaders themselves created. Reverse that dynamic through direct engagement and listening: not communicating through intermediaries and proxies about people who are not in the room.

As with most truly toxic behavior, one of the most important responsibilities of formal leadership, even in very horizontal and participatory organizations, is to protect the rights of individuals and the fundamental values of the organization's culture against abuse. This can be very challenging when the pressure to cast individual rights and collective values aside is coming from within the organization, perhaps even from a significant number of staff. Oppressive organizational cultures develop from below as often as from above—especially when leaders abdicate their responsibilities by failing to show courage in the face of toxic internal behavior.

The hardest job for any leader is to defend an organization from itself. However, moving toward fear, radical transparency, and willingness to engage will ensure that you'll be ready when the bell rings.

EPILOGUE

GREATNESS IS A HABIT NOT AN EVENT

When James "Buster" Douglas knocked out "Iron" Mike Tyson on February 11, 1990, it was arguably the greatest upset in the history of boxing. For Tyson, the fight was supposed to be a cake walk—just another human speed bump on Tyson's ferocious tear through the heavyweight division. However, Tyson's personal life had already started to unravel. Boxing has always helped to control Tyson's inner demons with an ultra-disciplined training regimen and coaches who provided him with father figures he respected. His coaches helped to tame the troubled soul of a young man who'd known tremendous pain, abandonment, and loss as a child. Boxing had given the young Tyson a potential way out of a life of violence and self-destruction. His natural aggression and physical ability, combined with a traumatic past and coaches like Cus D'Amato who were experts at turning "angry young men" into professional gladiators, made Tyson a once in a lifetime phenomenon. In his prime and at his best, Tyson had few equals in the history of boxing.

However, fame, money, power, and all that comes with it had begun to erode his disciplined lifestyle before that fateful night in February 1990. Most fans hadn't realized this at the time. To those of us who grew up in the '80s and '90s, Tyson was still an unstoppable freight train. His personal life was nothing to look up to, but his craft was simply unmatched. When you watched a Tyson fight on Pay-Per-View, you had to be careful not to take a bathroom break during the first round. He had multiple fights that lasted only seconds or minutes—capped by brutal one-sided knockouts. The Douglas fight was supposed to be an easy "tune-up" fight before Tyson fought real contenders in the coming year or two.

That was not to be. Douglas was renowned for having incredible natural ability, but he had never seemed to live up to his full potential. He lacked discipline. His performances were often erratic and inconsistent. Natural ability carried him far, but no one thought that he was poised to dethrone the ultimate "master of disaster," "Iron" Mike Tyson. Douglas realized this, and for multiple reasons that year decided to dig deep and find out, perhaps just this once, how good he really could be. In the lead up to this fight, Douglas trained like never before. He took advice from coaches and trainers that he had previously brushed off or implemented half-heartedly in the past. He decided that on that February night, the best Buster Douglas possible was going to walk into the ring. That's what he did, and that's how he won. He made a decision to believe in himself and, for the first time in his career, work as hard as a luminary like Tyson.

As usual, Tyson came out like bully in the first round. His style depended on winning as much through intimidation as through punching power. Douglas didn't back down and showed Tyson he wasn't afraid of him. This visibly threw off Tyson's game. Douglas stood up to the bully, and the bully cracked. Eventually, in the tenth round, Douglas knocked Tyson to the mat—*the first knockdown ever in Tyson's career.* Douglas followed up on the knockdown with a barrage of punishment. Then, to the astonishment of the world, Douglas knocked Tyson out. Few could believe it. The world was stunned. (Check out the book The Last Great Fight by Joe Layden for an in-depth discussion of the men and the circumstances that led to that fateful fight.)

Douglas proved that Tyson was not superhuman. He was just another guy. He had incredible natural abilities, to be sure, but he also worked harder than most of the people he fought. When Douglas matched Tyson's level of preparation, discipline, and work, he won. That's the lesson for us. We are capable of far more than we believe, which is actually kind of scary. That fact limits acceptable excuses for not reaching our goals. On the flip side, it means that preparation, discipline, and work are the real factors that separate pretenders and contenders. Life is too short to pretend. Let's get to work.

RECOMMENDED RESOURCES

INSPIRATION FROM THE LIVES OF REAL FIGHTERS

The Last Great Fight: The Extraordinary Tale of Two Men and How One Fight Changed Their Lives Forever, by Joe Layden

Harry Haft: Survivor of Auschwitz, Challenger of Rocky Marciano, by Alan Scott Haft

A Warrior's Heart: The True Story of Life Before and Beyond The Fighter, by Micky Ward with Joe Layden

Cus D'Amato: Life Lessons On Will, Skill, Discipline & Psychological Warfare From Mike Tyson's Mentor, by R. Shaw

The Cus D'Amato Mind: Learn the Simple Secrets That Took Boxers Like Mike Tyson to Boxing Greatness, by Reemus Boxing

LEADERSHIP AND PSYCHOLOGY

Antifragile: Things that Gain from Disorder, by Nassim Nicholas Taleb

The Black Swan: The Impact of the Highly Improbable, by Nassim Nicholas Taleb

Extreme Ownership: How U.S. Navy Seals Lead and Win, by Jocko Willink

The Human Side of Managing Technological Innovation: A Collection of Readings, by Ralph Katz

Shame and Pride: Affect, Sex, and the Birth of the Self, by Donald L. Nathanson

An Everyone Culture: Becoming A Deliberately Developmental Organization, by Robert Kegan and Lisa Laskow Lahey

ABOUT THE AUTHOR

John Bailie is an Executive Coach and Family Business Consultant with Compass Point Consulting, based in Bethlehem, Pennsylvania — helping family businesses grow and build legacies that last. Previously, he was the President of the International Institute for Restorative Practices (IIRP) Graduate School, where he helped to create an international professional development platform and an independent graduate school from the ground up. He and his colleagues facilitated the creation of an emerging social science devoted entirely to the study of relationships, community, and conflict management. He has taught leadership and conflict studies at Columbia University and his doctoral work focused on adult learning and change. He lives in Bucks County, Pennsylvania, with his wife Erin, their four children, and way too many farm animals and pets.

www.ingramcontent.com/pod-product-compliance
Lightning Source LLC
Chambersburg PA
CBHW072126270326
41931CB00010B/1689